T0064555

My Study

Bubba

authorHOUSE®

AuthorHouse™
1663 Liberty Drive
Bloomington, IN 47403
www.authorhouse.com
Phone: 1 (800) 839-8640

Published by AuthorHouse 09/16/2015

ISBN: 978-1-5049-2093-3 (sc)
ISBN: 978-1-5049-2092-6 (e)

Print information available on the last page.

Contents

About the Author

Bubba claims to be a common man, like the millions of people on this planet. The only difference, if any, is his passion for truth. Though a common man, in his career as a welder he was fortunate to visit many countries. In his travels, he met many people of many nations. A true joy, he claims, was to feel the love within the hearts of many. He truly enjoyed the different cultures and different ways of life, and the love expressed for others within each culture. He often was reminded that we are all God's children by creation, and he believes that God loves every one of us in equal value.

In his travels in Egypt, Traina could feel the love of God felt by many people of that nation. He has felt the compassion of men as they knelt and bowed down to the East; he praised their awareness of God. He has traveled to China and witnessed the love of God. He has been in the Buddhist temples. He has walked through Hindu temples, and he has visited the beautiful Vatican of Rome. He has witnessed the love of God by many, all around the globe. The question he has asked himself is this: Do we love God? God loves everyone on this planet. But do we truly love Him? Do we even know Him?

His thoughts and concerns for himself were also connected to the many people of many nations. His deepest concern was the reality of God, and the many religions of the world. He claims there is only one Almighty God, the Creator of all.

Introduction

In this little book, *My Study*, you will see many of the same scripture quotations used over and over again. Please be patient. In different chapters of *My Study*, when you see the same scripture mentioned, it is because I hope you will see a greater depth in the words each time you read them. I have read some scriptures over and over again for many years, and never had a clue of the true understanding. Sure, I thought I did, from the religious teachings of whatever church I was a part of. But, if I truly did not understand the scripture, and the elders of my church could not explain it, the meaning was explained as "a God thing." Read *My Study*. You may be amazed to find out who we truly are and what we believe, or should believe.

When we begin to read the Bible, we learn in the book of Genesis that God created the world in six days. This is truly backed up by the words of the prophet Isaiah in chapter 45 verses 5 through 7. The prophet Isaiah plainly states that God Almighty is the creator of all, and no one else. This is truth. But when we get to the book of John, chapter 1 verse 10 states that Jesus, the created Son of God, created the world, was in the world, and the world knew Him not. When we are very young, as babes in Christ, we have little knowledge of His Word. The scripture can be very confusing; parts of it can seem to be complete contradictions of other parts. Some of us may have a great deal of understanding of the Word of God, but we fail to realize that God knows all things before they ever exist in the mind of humankind. When we read scripture concerning the birth of Christ, we have confirmed in our minds the beginning of the life of Christ. The scriptures teach us that God knows all things before they ever exist in this world, even before the world was. Christ Jesus always existed in spiritual form. Christ was always the flesh or spiritual vessel to contain the fullness of the Almighty Holy Spirit. How can I say this? The Bible teaches us that Jesus is the Holy Spirit. He is the Word of God. John 1:1: "In the beginning was the Word and the Word was with God, and the Word was God" (KJV). The word is all power and authority. This, of course, would be God Almighty.

If we become involved with a religion, and have little knowledge of the Word of God, this religion, whatever it may be, will teach us the understandings of scripture according to that religion. If we have little knowledge of scripture, we may be convinced of their teachings. Therefore, we have not found truth for ourselves; we have found religious doctrines. The world is full of religion—Christian and non-Christian beliefs. The dictionary defines the word religion as one's belief of God, or worship of God or gods.

The Bible teaches in these many verses, to seek Him diligently. Hebrews 11:6: "- But without faith it is impossible to please Him: for he that cometh to God must believe that he is, and that he is a rewarder of them that diligently seek him" (KJV). Hebrews 12:15: "looking diligently lest any man fail of the Grace of God; lest any route of bitterness springing up trouble you, and thereby many be defiled." (KJV). 1 Peter 1:10: "Of which salvation the prophets have enquired and searched diligently, who prophesied of the grace that should come unto you:" (KJV). . Exodus 15:26:

"And said, if thou wilt diligently hearken to the voice of the Lord thy God, and wilt do that which is right in his sight, and wilt give ear to his commandments, and keep all his statues, I will put none of these diseases upon thee, which I have brought upon the Egyptians: for I am the Lord, that healeth thee" (KJV). To seek God diligently is to actually study the scriptures. To study the scriptures, we must look at various Bible translations. What I mean by this is that man's translation of scripture may not be perfect. But the Word of God as a whole is perfect. I compare many translated books of scripture. Just to mention a few, I use the King James Version, translated to English in 1611; the New King James Version of 1982; the New World Translation; the Geneva Bible, one of the earliest English translation, done in 1599; and The Interlinear Bible: Hebrew-Greek-English. I also use *The New Strong's Expanded Exhaustive Concordance of the Bible* and *The New Strong's Complete Dictionary of Bible Words*. This book contains the original meanings of over fourteen thousand biblical words.

Here are just a few examples of why we need to search multiple biblical translations. In the King James Version (KJV), and in most Christian Bibles, John 1:1 reads, "In the beginning was the Word and the Word was with God, and the Word was God." In the New World Translation (NWT), John 1:1 reads like this: "In the beginning, the Word was, and the Word was with God, and the Word was a god." Note that the NWT says "and the Word was *a god*," using lower case *g* for the word *god*. This is simply to say that Jesus was not God Almighty. 1 Timothy 3:16 of the King James Version reads like this: "And without controversy great is the mystery of godliness: God was manifest in the flesh, justified in the Spirit, seen of angels, preached unto the Gentiles, believed on in the world, received up into glory." Note that this scripture is plainly speaking of Jesus. But, it reads "*God* was manifest in the flesh" with a capital G. 1 Timothy 3:16 of the New World Translation reads like this: "Indeed, the sacred secret of this godly devotion is adamantly great: He was manifest in flesh, was declared righteous in spirit, appeared to Angels, was preached about among nations, was believed upon in the world, was received up in glory." This scripture is speaking of Jesus as well. This is rightfully so, because Jesus was the Word of God made flesh. Another thing to notice is the small letter *s* in the word *spirit*. By this, this biblical text is implying Jesus was not the Almighty Spirit of God made flesh, but another god. In the New King James Version, Isaiah 45:5 states, "I am the Lord, and there is no other; There is no God besides Me." This informs us that there is no other God. In the King James Version, Isaiah 45:5 states, "There is no God beside me." This could be to literally inform us that there is no other God to His left or His right. In The Interlinear Bible: Hebrew-Greek-English, Isaiah 45:5 reads, "I am Jehovah, and there is none else; there is no God except me." In the New World Translation Isaiah 45:5 reads, "I am Jehovah, and there is no one else. With the exception of me, there is no God." Now one might ask, why do I nitpick over these verses? Well, in the English language it is commonly understood that, if I said, "there's no one besides me that can do something," then it is only I who can do it. If I were speaking to someone and I said, "There is no one beside me, I am alone," this is well understood! But, by the many translations of scripture, and the many religious doctrines, these two words, *besides* and *beside*, can make a great difference in biblical understanding. We cannot read one specific scripture and receive total understanding. All scripture together is taught in full value of its contents; this is our understanding. We must find the true understanding of scripture through all scripture.

Here are just a few more examples of why we need to search many Bible texts. In the King James Version, my favorite biblical text, I was very disappointed to find the word *Easter* in acts 12:4. The word *Easter*, in my opinion, is not the correct word to use for the time of Passover, although in this day and age, we commonly call this time of year Easter. This, in my opinion, shows me that man's translation is not always completely what it should be. But the Word of God as a whole is perfect! In the New King James Version, Acts 12:4 is translated correctly in my opinion. It reads like this: "So when he had arrested Him, he put Him in prison, and delivered Him to four squads of soldiers to keep Him, intending to bring Him before the people after Passover." The King James Version and the New King James Version often differ in word choice, and many other Bible texts differ from them. I caught this one in the Gospel of Luke during Bible study one Sunday. Luke 22:31–32, of the New King James Version. It reads like this: "And the Lord said, Simon, Simon! Indeed, Satan has asked for you, that he may sift you as wheat. But I have prayed for you, that your faith should not fail; and when you *have returned to me*, strengthen your brother." In the King James Version, Luke 22:31–32 reads like this: "And the Lord said, Simon, Simon, behold, Satan hath desired to have you, that he may sift you as wheat: but I have prayed for thee, that thy faith fail not: and *when thou art converted*, strengthen thy brethren." Okay, these two scriptures do differ. The New King James Version uses, in verse 32, the words *returned to me*. In the King James Version, verse 32 uses the words *when thou art converted*. Okay, this may not seem to be a big issue with many people, but I personally believe that it is.

If you look up the word *converted*, or *to convert*, in *The New Strong's Complete Dictionary of Bible Words*, the word *convert* is defined as "to turn back; to return, to revert, turned back to." The word *converted* is defined as "to turn about or over, to turn back; to return, to turn a round or reverse." In the *Webster's New World Dictionary*, the word *convert* is defined as "to return, to change, transformed, to change from one religion doctrine to another, to exchange for something equal in value, to be converted, a person converted, as to a religion." I will personally add that to be converted is to realize that what you once thought was truth is now of no value to you. To be converted is to suddenly realize the reality of truth by the existence of what is. Therefore, truth is of great value. It cannot be removed or altered. Truth is everlasting. This would mean you would turn around in your thoughts of life—convert, or reverse, or go in the opposite direction. Don't follow the cares of this world, but reverse your thoughts and actions, and head in the direction of Christ's everlasting life. So what is truth? Let's take a look at John 15:26: "But when the Comforter is come, whom I will send unto you from the Father, even the Spirit of truth, which proceeded from the Father, he shall testify of me: [Jesus]" (KJV). And who was Jesus? John 18:37: "Pilate therefore said unto him, Art thou a king then? Jesus answered, Thou sayest that I am a king. To this end was I born, and for this cause came I into the world, that I should bear witness unto the truth. Everyone that is of the truth heareth my voice" (KJV). So who is truth? According to John 15:26, it is Jehovah God, our Father in Heaven. Who was a witness of the truth? Why, of course Jesus, because He is the Word of God made flesh. This is why He says, "Everyone that is of the truth heareth my voice." *The voice of God!*

So here is what I am leading up to concerning the verses of Luke 22:31–32. If you read only the text of the New King James Version, you may never understand the truth of that scripture. In the King James Version, by reading the word *converted*, we will plainly see the truth of scripture unfolding some seventeen years after Jesus had told Simon Peter, "When thou art converted." Peter and all the disciples who were still alive and had walked with Jesus did not understand or believe the Grace-Age gospel of the apostle Paul (whose name was changed from Saul; see Acts 13:9). It had been approximately three years or better from that time Jesus spoke with Peter at the Last Supper. The apostle Paul had gone to Jerusalem to speak with Peter concerning the revelations of Christ given to the apostle Paul, after he had been blinded on the road to Damascus. Peter did not want to have any part of the teachings of Paul. Paul's teachings by the revelation of Christ were in direct conflict to the doctrines taught by the Jewish forefathers. Paul had left Jerusalem and had gone to preach throughout the known world—the gospel of grace. Paul had established many churches. Then, after fourteen years, he returned to Jerusalem to speak with Peter once again. This is when Peter finally understood the words of Paul from the revelation of Christ. This is when Peter was finally converted, and persuaded his brothers to believe the Grace Age gospel, the gospel of Christ. You may find this truth in the book of Acts. You may start at chapter 9, but this is confirmed in chapters 1 and 2 in the book of Galatians.

In this little book, *My Study*, I am not claiming to know all biblical truths. The truth of the matter is, I don't know very much at all. But what I do know, I know that I know! What is written in this book may stem from religious knowledge given to me from various religious doctrines, when I began to seek Him diligently after years and countless hours of study. The scripture became very clear in my mind. As I read and studied the scripture, I learned to put my religious doctrines back in the box they had come out of. Even though many were justified by scripture, all were not fully explained in the entirety of truth. Through the years I have been a member of a few religious doctrines. These, of course, would be so-called churches. I say this so that I can define the church. We, as believers in Christ Jesus our Lord and Savior, are the church! The buildings we may attend on Sundays are merely places to congregate as the church.

As a Christian, I feel it is my duty to share my thoughts and understanding of scripture. This little book, *My Study*, is exactly what the title indicates: my personal study. With all honesty, I have to say these are my opinions. As it is in all religions of the world, Christian or non-Christian, one's thoughts are merely one's opinion. The Word of God teaches us in Philippians 2:12 that we must work out our own salvation with fear and trembling. I take this as a serious matter. By following a religion blindly, rather than seeking Him diligently for yourself, you may be placing your life— your everlasting life—in the hands of a deceiver. It may not be the person or persons deceiving you, but the spirit of deception. I'm not saying your religion, or any religion, Christian or non-Christian, is completely wrong about God and the ideas pertaining to God. In my opinion, all religions of the world teach truth and error. What I am saying is, get out of your religious box. Just stick your head out of the box. You don't have to leave. But, if you close the box because you feel very comfortable, and continue to hit the four walls of doctrine, which are your religious teachings of scripture, you may be deceived. I don't know. I'm not God. But I do have my head out of the box and my ears are open. I am always willing to listen to anyone's point of view about his or her beliefs. Then I will go to the scripture to confirm or disprove. This is all I'm asking anyone to do. I'm not asking anyone to leave his or her religion. I am not offering you another religion based on my thoughts and words and opinions. I am asking only that you accept the knowledge of the Word of God. I am asking only that you accept the offer that Jesus is offering. This would be a true and intimate relationship with our Father of Heaven, and not just a ritual of religious acts and doctrines. If you truly believe you have truth, then nothing I say can move you. The truth is solid; it cannot be moved.

If you will read *My Study*, it will become your study. You may truly begin to seek Him diligently. You must have a pad and pen at hand. Write down your disagreements; you have a God-given right to disagree. But, for the sake of truth or opinions, which are many, please read the entire book. Either prove me wrong in my thoughts, or let them be confirmed. I heard this said once, and I love it: "I boldly stand to humbly be corrected." Isn't that beautiful? Know this—I boldly stand in the Word of God for truth! Also know this—I will humbly kneel for correction. We must believe in what we will believe. But if we are proven wrong by the Word of God, we must surrender to His Word.

Praise be to God.

My Testimony

"First remember this!" I *do* mean remember it! If my sin is greater than yours, or if yours is greater than mine, what's the difference? Sin is sin, and sin leads to death. The Bible teaches us that a little leaven *spoils* the whole loaf.

Now, a bit of information about the one who has penned this little book. My friends and family call me Bubba—just a common name for a common man. When I say common, I mean just that. I am no different from any of the millions of people who walk this planet. We all have one thing in common. This common issue may result in death or lead to everlasting life. I am sixty-three years old, and I have reached this age only by the grace of God. My first forty years were carefree and all about me. For the first two-thirds of my life, I truly lived in blind faith. Yes, I was blind to the Word of God. Sure, I went to church; I went to many different churches. To my understanding, in those days, this is where I would find God. To my disappointment, I did not truly find Him. I did learn more about Him, but I did not know Him. We sometimes follow a Christian religion with what I may call a blind faith. Here is an example. We read in the Bible, "Thou shalt not covet." But on Friday or Saturday night, we go out to a bar to find someone who is willing to help fulfill our fleshly lust. If we can do this, then we are living in blind faith.

The Bible teaches that God is all loving, all knowing, all merciful, and all forgiving. This we can understand very quickly in any Christian religion. The Bible also teaches that

Jesus is our Savior, and that the ones who believe in Him shall be saved. This we really grab hold of as truth. This is so easily understood. The Bible states in 2 Corinthians 3:3, "Forasmuch as ye are manifestly declared to be the epistle of Christ ministered by us, written not with ink, but with the Spirit of the living God; not in tables of stone, but in fleshy tables of the heart" (KJV). This in my opinion is that He will put His commandments in our hearts on fleshly tablets, not on tablets of stone." If we cannot understand this passage from the scriptures and truly live by it, then we are living in blind faith.

I had lived a life of sin—lived it willingly and boldly. Yet I would claim the love of God. This was true. Even then, God did love me, but did I love Him? Did I truly know Him? I think not! How could I have truly known Him when I lived a life in fulfillment of fleshly desires?

I was a true party animal in my youth. If possible, I found a way to go out every night. My thoughts were to work hard in the day and to play hard at night—burning the candle at both ends. Yet in those days, even as a man full of the lust of life, I knew God loved me, and I felt He would forgive me. I knew just enough of the love of God to keep me content in my sinful way of life. I was never one who deliberately would cause trouble for anyone, or who spoke badly of anyone. I don't ever remember having feelings of jealousy or envy toward anyone, perhaps because I was content in who I was. I worked hard to get everything in life I wanted. If there were things I could not afford, I simply forgot about them. But if I could buy something, it was mine. I worked hard and honestly for everything in life. If I told you something, you could take it to the bank, as we say. I guess this is why I thought I was a "good old boy" or as more commonly said, a "good person."

In reality, I was anything but good, especially when it came to women. Don't get me wrong. I had then—and still have—the utmost respect for women. Other than the ultimate gift of salvation, I believe woman is the greatest and most beautiful gift God gave man. She is the fulfillment of man. A man should place a woman above himself, high up on a pedestal. I have always had these feelings. But, in my youth, lacking true love for God and only somewhat knowing the love of God, I found that my respect for women could fail quickly.

I never was one to physically abuse a woman—never. Lord forgive me, I know I have mentally abused three women in my life. These were my second, third, and fourth wives. I am married now to my fourth wife. My first wife and I were very young and naive. Neither of us understood the values of life. How could we? We were both just teenagers, wanting to live as mature adults. When we are young, we sometimes make foolish mistakes that carry everlasting consequences. The fact that we were so young and blind to the reality of life meant that our decisions led us to the destruction of our marriage. Even though I still had love for her, we divorced. Shortly after my first divorce, I enlisted in the army.

After serving three years and developing many bad habits, I found my views of life had changed. I no longer felt the need for a true relationship with a woman. There was no longer any need within me to give respect to a woman, mainly because I had none for myself, just as a woman likely had none for herself. This was back in the early 1970s when many of us were looking for love in all the wrong places. After a few years of this sinful way of life, I was awakened to my memory of the love of God. I had developed a lot of bad habits in my time of service, although, when I was in the army, I first began to read the Holy Bible, the Word of God. You might ask what happened, and ask me, "If you read the Bible and felt the love of God, why did you live such a sinful life?" The only honest answer I can give you is this: I didn't understand one word of the Bible, but I did know the lust of life. I didn't think I was a bad person. I was doing only what is natural for any young man; that is, any young man without the Spirit of God dwelling in him. I didn't know it at the time, but the first is the natural man. Then, once he is born again, the spiritual man comes. This would not become a reality with me for many years.

In my years of wandering in life as a lost sheep, I became a heavy drinker. Alcohol had become my sedative to numb the thoughts and emotions of a very confused young man. Sure, on the outside it appeared as if I truly had it together. I had a good job, worked hard, and acquired in life all the fine things any young person could hope for. I had nice clothes, jewelry, a fine car, money in the bank, and money in my pocket.

As time went on, alcohol no longer had the power to numb the thoughts and emotions of a confused young man. In fact, alcohol had now become my greater problem. I knew my life had to change. As time went on, in this great mystery of life, with a future unknown, I struggled with my thoughts and emotions. Where is God? Who is God? In fact, who am I, and why am I here? I thought perhaps I had lost my purpose in life when I lost my first love, a love I had felt was real and worthy of 100 percent of all I had within me. As a young and foolish man, I knew nothing of the mysteries of life.

Beaten down to the level of disgust, I turned to the Word of God once again. My thoughts, even in the most sinful time of my life, focused on asking, "What can I know of the existence of God? Who is He?" I began to think about scripture, the scripture I did understand. I began to feel I could not be complete without love and a relationship with one woman. Nothing changed in my life for at least two more years. I continued on with my sinful way of life. Yes, I did read the Bible and tried to understand it, but this happened for the most part only when I was down in my thoughts of life.

Then, one night in a bar, I met a woman through a friend of mine. I was attracted to her. We began to date. As our relationship grew stronger, I began to think, *Could this woman be the one I could share my life with?* It wasn't long before those feelings were almost destroyed. Early in our relationship, something happened that would dismantle the trust I had built in her. We were apart for a while. So I returned to alcohol and women as the fulfillment for the emptiness within. I didn't know it was God I needed, and I had no real clue of what He could do for me.

After some time of being apart, we met and spoke about our problems. Knowing I was not happy with my life, and feeling a second chance with her might prove to be the right decision, I gave it another chance. After all, I had given my first wife this opportunity. This would prove to be the wrong decision. Unsure of marriage, we married anyway. I told a close cousin of mine that, if this marriage didn't work, I'd just get a divorce. That, of course, was not the will of God. After four and a half years of marriage and a daughter, I'd had enough. In the beginning of the marriage, I lost a great deal of respect for her. Even though I felt compassion and love for her, I did not have much respect for those feelings. Our views of life and the reality of God were as far apart as the East is from the West. We had absolutely nothing in common, so I divorced her. Alcohol was once again the only way I could deal with another failure. From the beginning to the end of that marriage, alcohol was always present. The alcohol, the harsh words, and my actions of no respect toward a woman who claimed to love me were all unjustifiable. The mental abuse she received from me was undeserved. We were simply two people who saw life from much different perspectives. Though I thought in the beginning that we might come together as one in the knowledge of who we were, and who God is, this reality, of course, could not happen. Why? I know now it was my lack of knowledge of the Word of God.

Life went on, and so did my consumption of alcohol and my thoughts of life. I turned to the Word of God once more, but it wasn't until I had become attached to a young lady I had known for quite some time. She was eleven and a half years younger than I. She was about to turn nineteen; I was thirty. As time went on, we became quite close in friendship.

One night when we were talking, she leaned forward and kissed me. This, of course, was the beginning of another failure, which would come four and a half years later. I had known her before the divorce of my second wife, and now was dating her before my divorce was final. Out of the frying pan and into the fire, as we say. Nevertheless, I was determined to have a one-woman relationship, with God, and the knowledge of God in our lives. She agreed.

Shortly after that, we were invited to attend church with one of my friends from work. We both were a little reluctant to go. This church was quite different in their religious teachings and actions of worship than the church we had been brought up in. I knew my friend was a man of God. What I mean by that is, he knew God, and the understanding of His Word. He seemed to be very stable in life, and headed in one direction. We decided to attend the church. Things were strange at first, but the more we went, the more we understood the Word of God. Or so I thought. We had come to a point of knowledge in God's Word that we could no longer share our intimate expressions of love in a physical expression of love for one another. This, of course, was not easy, but we did it.

Even though I was eleven and a half years her senior, I began to think once again, *Is she the one?* Some months later, my divorce from my second wife was final. Now free to marry once again, I married this young lady, who had followed me down this very difficult trail. We had come together in the knowledge of God. We were happy with our church and our lives together. Sometime later, we were invited to a barbecue at a church friend's house. I didn't know it at the time, but this visit would be the end of my religious views, and the beginning of the failure of my third marriage. At the barbecue, I heard a man speaking to my church friends. He was not a member of our church, but of the same faith. I heard him say that the people of my church were all going to hell. His reason? We were all too worldly. This statement hit me hard and caused me to go into deep thought. I knew who I had been before I had become a member of this church. I had been a man of the world. I had experienced many sinful thoughts and actions. I was an alcoholic, I had chased women, I had smoked cigarettes, and I had used profanity as common language. Most of all, I had learned no true knowledge and understanding of God's Word. Now that I was a member of this church, and the Word of God was fed to me daily, my life had truly changed, and I had been cleansed of all these evil deeds.

I knew I had truly received a spiritual gift from God. I began to think deeply of what I had been taught through the Word of God, and the understanding of it from that church. I realized through much thought that I was no different than this man who had condemned us. I knew I also was judging others. I saw everyone outside of my church headed for hell. I didn't realize it at the time, but I was still a sinner. Sure, I knew God had changed me, but I was no different than anyone else, capable of sin. Because of the love and concern for others, which comes from the knowledge of God, we sometimes ignorantly condemn others. Why? It is from a lack of understanding of God's Word. Sure, we can rightfully judge sin, because it is the choice of knowledge of good and evil, but we must never condemn someone because of sin—even as a Christian, or should I say, more so as a Christian. We should not judge others who are living in sin. Why? Because we are all sinners, and sin leads to death. We all deserve to die. From the knowledge of God's Word, and the death, burial, and resurrection of Jesus Christ, we are saved by grace and nothing else.

Well, like I said, I didn't understand scripture as I do now. That's not to say I know a whole lot, but what I do know, I know! After thinking of what was said that day, and knowing somehow that something was wrong, I knew what he'd said was not of God; neither were my thoughts about other people outside my church of God. I began to lose faith in my church. I did not lose faith in God, only religion. I could see now that all religions of this world claim to have the truth about God, and the knowledge of how to worship Him. I'd had enough of religion. I knew God was real, and He loved me, but I was very confused. We left that church and slowly became comfortable in living apart from His Word (the knowledge of the Bible). I didn't know it at the time, but God did not leave me. He held me in His hand, and no one could pluck me from it. As our lives together grew further from the Word of God, we drifted from the knowledge of God, who at one time had been the center of our relationship. The Word of God was no longer the foundation of our relationship. This, of course, led us down a road of destruction.

Alcohol had now become a sedative once more for a very troubled mind and soul. As the months and years had passed, so had the hope of a true relationship. We both may have shared the guilt of mental abuse, but I'm sure mine was greater than hers. After four and a half years, once again, my marriage was over. We divorced. Our lives together did not end there, however. I'm not truly sure why, other than the fact that we had gone through a spiritual change of life. Now that we were back living a destructive lifestyle, I agreed to live with her as a couple once again. Now divorced, but living with a woman, I was living a life not in favor of God or man. After a few months of this useless effort to have some sort of a relationship together, she asked, "If we were to have a child, would you marry me again?" This brought great thought and worry to my mind. At this point in our lives, I was very unsure of all things in our relationship. She wanted an answer. I could not give her a quick and honest answer, so I simply said no. This, of course, to her, was the wrong answer. The only sure thing about my answer was the end of that relationship forever.

Now I was alone once again, troubled deeply in mind, heart and soul, and alcohol became a sedative once more. Even so, God was constantly on my mind. God had given me a spiritual gift. Though I had prayed for weeks, with occasional fasting, the night I received this spiritual gift, I had totally not expected it. I had not forgotten this: I knew God was with me, and His Word was solid. Though I had lost my faith in religion, my faith in God and His Word was etched deeply in my spirit. I did try once more with an organized religion, but after only eight weeks, that too was a total wash. I knew then, if I was ever going to understand who God truly is, and what His Word truly teaches, I needed to study it for myself.

Life went on for perhaps a year and a half, and so did my thoughts of God, and my sinful actions of man. I was not happy with my life. I truly was not looking for a woman to share my life with, but I somehow felt that, if I had someone, I could settle down, quit going to the bars, and devote more time to God. (This, of course, was foolish thinking.) It must be a one-on-one relationship with God, our Father in Heaven. It doesn't matter if you are married or single. It is still a one-on-one relationship. I didn't realize or understand this truth until after four years into the marriage of my present fourth wife. When I met my wife, she was beautiful, inside and out. She was very sweet and easy to get along with. Though she had no real knowledge of God's Word, I thought I could teach her what I thought I knew. Looking back, I didn't know very much at all. Even now I feel I have merely broken the ice to the wisdom and knowledge of God's Holy Word.

In the beginning of our marriage, everything was wonderful. I had now begun to actually study the Bible. I would listen to as many preachers on radio and television as I could. It wasn't religion I was after; it was the understanding of God's Word. I was listening to the radio one afternoon, and heard that a preacher I was familiar with was coming to my area. I had heard him preach many times. I was very interested in his views and how he understood the Word of God. I decided to go and hear him preach. Before I left there, I was able to speak with him for a while. I told him I had an interest in the Word of God. I told him I read and studied the Bible, but I just didn't understand the message. Well, he laughed at me—not in a bad way, but in a way that showed he was not surprised. He said, "Son, just keep reading, studying, and searching. You will understand." He did give me incentive and a hope that I would truly learn to understand. Now, twenty-three years later, I can truly understand that preachers words. The Bible says in Hebrews 11:6, seek God diligently (KJV). Like everything in life, it is work. Much time and effort must be spent for anything we wish to obtain in this life. Learning and understanding the Word of God is no different. You reap what you sow, as the Bible puts it. Give it all you can, and, for your efforts, you will receive all you can.

Four years into our marriage, my wife showed little interest in the Word of God. This disturbed me greatly. I felt we had to be together in search of knowledge of God's Word. This, of course, was foolish, but I felt that, if my wife wasn't with me, then she was against me. I began to see things differently in our marriage. I began to see things in her that I had seen in the women of my past. I began to feel a lack of respect for her, as I felt she lacked respect for me. These fleshly emotions of torment had hindered my spiritual yearning for the Word of God. Our marriage was quite rocky and not so wonderful at times. If my wife had not been the woman she is, our marriage would have been over. She put up with my unstable thoughts and emotions. My life was like a roller coaster up and down. I didn't realize it then, but I strongly felt my wife had to feel the same for the Word of God as I did. This again was foolish! It wasn't until I truly understood what it meant to put the Lord first, then I would receive peace. The Bible teaches us to love Him more than our mother, father, sister, or brother. This is only to understand that it is a one-on-one relationship—you and God! Once we realize this, we can truly give our lives to Christ. That is to say, "Lord Jesus, you take control. I cannot do anything with my life except to make a mess of it. I surrender to you, Lord Jesus." Then, He is your Lord—not just *the* Lord, but *your* Lord! Once I understood this truth, it was in my heart. Now I was finally able emotionally to seek Him diligently. Nothing else mattered! If my wife, or anyone else, disagreed or showed little interest in the Word of God, it didn't matter. Sure, my concerns for them were still there, but my relationship and knowledge of God's Word came first. Then I could relax in my thoughts of concern for my wife and others. It was all in the hands of God. I thank God my wife is the woman she is. If she had been any different, I don't think I could possibly say we have been married now for twenty-five years. We have hosted Bible study at our home now for over three years. She is right there beside me. This is the will of God!

Praise be to God.

The Mystery of the Spirit

I am like a hound in a hot and determined pursuit after the scent of truth, baying at the base of a great tree, howling, with my front claws deeply buried within its bark. As I look up in direction of the hidden scent, I am blinded by its great canopy of cover. The scent of truth is here; I know it is. I have followed it step by step. As I howl in excitement, my tail wags swiftly with joy. I wonder at the mystery high above. Is it here? Is it truly here? Have I truly found it at last?

Then a thought occurs as I look around in the darkness of night. I have followed my nose with great faith in the scent. But as I look in the darkness through trees, I see that there are many. The scent is high above in the mystery of cover. I wonder, *am I barking up the wrong tree?*

Well, as a man, not a hound, I think not. I have followed scripture, which is the light of the world. I am not in the darkness of many denominational teachings. But don't take my word for truth! Study the Word of God. This would be the Holy Bible. Study and learn for yourself the mysteries that are hidden from the carnal mind. We must be born again—born once born of the flesh, but then we must be born of the Spirit of God, our Father—brought to us by Jesus the Christ.

Praise be to God.

He, God Almighty

First let me say this: In this life on planet Earth, we are in the physical realm. We truly can understand this physical realm for what is. Science proves this physical realm in many ways.

What some of us may not fully realize is that there is a spiritual realm as well. Furthermore, this spiritual realm is the true existence of what is, in the physical realm. Here is an example of what I'm saying: for man to invent, or create, the creation must exist in his mind, or the spiritual realm, first. In this world, the physical realm, there are many languages. These languages consist of words. When words exist in thought or mind, they do not exist in the physical realm. When they are written so one can see them, they are in the physical realm. With that said, realize that written words first had to exist in the spiritual realm. They were in your mind, in your emotions, and it was your will to express them in the physical realm—whether it be the spirit of the world, or in the Spirit of Christ. With that said, remember that God is the invisible, Almighty Spirit. He, with His Word, literally *spoke* everything into existence. Therefore, the Spirit of God is now in, and of, the physical world. His Words spoken are the existence of what is. The proof of His spiritual Words, from the mind, the emotions, and the will of God, exist now as this physical realm; they are the existence of what is, as the Word of God.

If you think my understanding of the physical and spiritual realms is nonsense, read more of *My Study* or, most importantly, read the Holy Bible. This is the only way one can truly understand who He, Almighty God, is. With that said, let's take a look at some physical knowledge brought from the spiritual realm by physical words written from the minds and emotions expressed through the will of humankind.

If you like history, but are not aware of this truth expressed by the words of history, you may be quite amazed at this truth. Many are totally unaware of this knowledge. If you are aware, you may still be amazed at the knowledge of this truth. First, remember this—we live in a very sinful world, an imperfect world, only because of sin. In this sinful world, I have heard the Holy and precious name of Jesus used by humankind in a very sinful and filthy way. With that said, what does history tell us about the name *Jesus*?

Go online and type this into the Google search bar: "What is the true name for Jesus?" Then diligently research this subject. You may be shocked by some of the remarks pertaining to the name *Jesus*. The remarks I mention here are just a few of many. Some claim the true name in Aramaic was *Isa*, but pronounced as *Esa*. Some believe the true Hebrew name for Jesus is *Zeus*. This, of course, if you are a Christian, sounds like a very pagan connection. Many believe the original Hebrew and Aramaic translation would be *Yehoshu'a*. The short form of this name would be *Yeshu'a* or *Joshua*. (This would be like saying *Dave* for *David* in English.) The Hebrew name *Yeshu'a*, in Greek, was once written as *Iesous*. It was also known in Latin as *Iesus*. Then through the centuries it was changed from the name *Iesus* to what we now know—*Jesus*.

There may be many reasons for the many names for Jesus. The most evident I found was online in the *Encyclopedia Americana*, in which I found this quote pertaining to the letter *J*: "The form of Jay was unknown in any alphabet until the 14th century. Either symbol (J, I) used initially generally had the consonantal sound of Y, as in year. Gradually, the two symbols (J, I) were differentiated, the J usually acquiring consonantal force and thus becoming a vowel. It was not until 1630 that the differentiation became general in English. In the original 1611 version of the King James Version of the Bible, there was no letter *J* because it did not exist. James was spelled *Iames*. Jesus was spelled *Iesous.*"

This information above found in the Encyclopedia Americana, would most likely also apply for the name *Jehovah*, as Jehovah God. Remember, in the original scripture of the ancient Hebrew and Aramaic language, there was no *J*. The letters *J* and *I* were pronounced *ya*, as in *Yahweh*, the name used by the Hebrews for the one and only God. These two letters looked very much like a modern day *J* or I simply were pronounced *ya*. Note: it is not clear to me from the articles I've read, but it could be the letter *J* is not used in the Hebrew language to this very day. You may research this for yourself.

The most important thing I have deduced from this information—the way I see it—is that *y-a-h* are the first three letters in the word *Yahweh*, which is the Hebrew word for God. The last three letters found in the word *hallelujah*, of the ancient Hebrew and Aramaic languages, would have most certainly been *y-a-h*. With this knowledge, let's see how the *Webster's New World Dictionary* defines *hallelujah*:

"praise, thanks, etc., of praise to God." In my opinion, in the Hebrew language, this could simply mean, praise be to God—*Hallel Yah*.

All this knowledge in differences of language and alphabets, in my opinion, makes no difference. The important thing is what we believe in our spirit in Christ Jesus. Remember, the world is a sinful and evil place because of sin—Satan. He is in the world to destroy, to confuse, and to dismantle the Word of God. He has done so by being a deceiving spirit. He has accomplished this through the many religions of the world—both Christian and non-Christian belief systems. Christians believe that Satan has come to confuse the Word and dismantle the Word of God. How and why? In my opinion, because of the many denominational teachings and belief systems that try to teach us how to understand scripture, either by truth or error. All religions of the world have truth and error. Satan has performed his duty well. I feel that the truth of Jesus—His name—is not in the physical realm, but in the spiritual realm. That is where we can find knowledge of who He truly is. Although the name of Jesus is above all names, remember, He will reveal an unknown name for the completion; in other words, eternity. Read Revelations 19:12 in any Christian bible.

The point is this in my opinion: In the physical realm, the people who love me know me as Bubba, but Bubba is not my given name. Whether I am called Bubba, or my given name, this is not who I truly am. Whatever name is used, it only identifies the physical body or vessel, which contains my spirit, which is my true identity. This is how I see the reality of the physical Son of God. He was physical as Jesus, but all scripture teaches us that He was the Almighty Spirit, the Word of God, as the Christ, the only anointed begotten of the flesh, which is the physical realm. In the words of scripture—the Bible—Jesus expresses His true identity in numerous quotes in the gospels. The words of John 10:30 are most evident, as they read, "I and my Father are one." Jesus was not speaking of the physical realm as His body. He was speaking only about the Spirit, the Almighty Spirit, which He contained in that body. This would be the true identity of Jesus— He, Almighty God! Go to the gospel of John 5:43. If is not clear to you, read the whole chapter.

To truly believe scripture as the Word of God would be to intimately know His Spirit. This would be our Father God, He, Almighty God! Jesus is the "He," in the scripture Deuteronomy 32:39, in any Christian Bible.

In all Christian belief we know and say there is but one God. The Bible teaches us that God Almighty is Spirit (John 4:24 KJV). Yet some of us believe in a trinity. Some Christian believers say there are three individual beings: God the Father, God the Son, and God the Holy Spirit. The Bible says in Deuteronomy 32:39, "see now that I, even I am he, and there is no god with me" (KJV). The Bible says, or indicates, that God Almighty sits on His throne, and His Son Jesus is at His right hand. This we read as truth. So where is the Holy Spirit? Perhaps at His left hand? Isaiah 45:18: "I am the Lord, and there is none else" (KJV). This is true. There is but one God, and the Bible teaches us that He is Spirit (John 4:24 KJV). I believe and know with all my heart that there is only one God.

We all know in this great nation of America: United we stand, separate we fall. Well, Satan knows this also. Not only is America a country in a fallen state, but her churches are fallen as well. Why? Because the so-called churches of America are full of blindness. Yes, they are blind—blind to the Word of God. This didn't just start to come about. This started long ago, just after the death, burial, and resurrection of Jesus Christ. Sin has always been in the world as we say, but the spirit of the antichrist came quickly to confuse and dismember the Word of God.

Most people believe their religion, or faith, is their church. One may also believe that salvation comes only from within that so-called church. No, we as believers, *are* the church! No matter what faith we have, the truth is the Word of God. We must read and understand it well.

If you think deeply about the scripture you are reading, it will make spiritual and scriptural sense. The Word must be with God as one, because the Word is all knowledge and power. I will give you an example of how the word *with* means "as one," and not "alongside of." This may sound a little off base, but please be patient, read *My Study* in its entirety, then you may see my point.

As we may have learned in school, red, yellow, and blue are the primary colors. Yellow with blue makes green, red with yellow makes orange, and orange with blue makes brown. All primary colors together make black. White is the absence of color. Realize now that God is the author of all things. If yellow with blue—together—are one, so is flesh and spirit. In reference to Jesus, He is the anointed flesh vessel, created as the Son of God, filled with the fullness of God's Spirit (Colossians 2:9 and John 3:34, read any Christion bible). I see them totally as one. The New World Translation of John 1:1 reads, "In the beginning the Word was, and the Word was with God, and the Word was a god." John 1:2 of the New World Translation reads, "This one was in the beginning with God." John 1:3 of the New World Translation reads, "All things came into existence through him, and apart from him, not even one thing came into existence." I see the New World Translation using the word *with* as we might say "alongside of" God. If this is true, then all scripture of the New World Translation would accurately mesh perfectly together with other scripture translations of that Bible. I am sorry to say in my opinion, it does not! The King James Version and the New World Translation each teaches me one solid understanding of the Bible, but this, of course, ignores the word changes in the New World Translation.

Notice that in all three scriptures, Jesus is known as the Word. This is rightfully so, but if God our Father is Almighty, surely it is His Word. So the Word was in the beginning with God as one, then and now, and always! No word, no God! In *My Study*, you will hopefully see the scriptures that will explain my explanations.

God, who always was, was never alone in His thoughts of creation. Just keep this in mind as you read *My Study*.

Praise be to God.

Jesus Said

Note: all of the scriptures in this section come from the King James Version (italics are mine). You may compare them with any Bible texts.

John 10: 30: "I, and my Father are one."

John 8:19: "Ye neither knew me, nor my Father: if you had known me, ye should have known my Father *also*."

John 6:38: "For I came down from Heaven, not to do *mine* own will, but the will *of him* that sent me."

John 2:16: Take these things hence, make not *my Father's house* an house of merchandise."

John 3:16: "For *God* so loved the world, that he gave his only begotten *son*, that whosoever believeth in him should not perish, but have everlasting life."

John 4:24: "God is Spirit, and they that worship him must worship him in spirit and in truth."

John 5:22: "*For the Father* judges no man, but has committed all judgment unto the Son:"

John 6:29: "This is the work *of God*, that ye *believe on him* whom he hath sent."

John 7:16: "My doctrine is *not mine*, but *his that sent me*."

John 6:46: "Not that any man hath seen the Father, save he which is of God, he hath seen the Father."

John 6:65: "Therefore said I unto you, that no man can come unto me, except it were given unto him of my Father."

John 8:29: "And he that sent me is with me: the Father hath not left me alone; for I do always those things that please him."

John 10:36: "Because I said, I am the son of God."

John 10:38: "Believe, that the *Father is in me, and I in him*."

John 11:41: "Father, I thank thee that thou hast heard me."

John 12:50: "I speak therefore, even as the Father said unto me, so I speak."

John 13:16: "Verily, verily, I say unto you, The servant is not greater than his Lord, neither he that is sent greater than he that sent him."

John 13:31: "Now is the Son of man glorified, and God is glorified in him."

John 13:32: "If God be glorified in him, God shall also glorify him in himself, and shall straightway glorify him."

John 12:44: "He that believeth on me, believeth not on me, but on him that sent me."

John 14:23: "If a man love me, he will keep my words: and my Father will love him, and we will come unto him, and make our abode with him."

John 17:22: "And the glory which thou gavest me I have given them; that they may be one, even as we are one." (Note: this scripture is speaking of Spirit, one, in the **Almighty** Spirit of God our Father!)

Now I know that, just by reading a little of what Jesus said, you may be confused. You might ask, "Is He God?" Plainly, He is always asking of the Father, praying to the Father, or hearing from the Father—then acting upon the Father's will.

Okay, better yet, what about these three scriptures?

John 10:30: "I and my Father are one."

John 12:45: "And he that seeth me, seeth him that sent me."

Matthew 27:46: "My God, my God, why hast thou forsaken me?"

This is all understood only by the spiritual knowledge, and understanding of all scripture. Keep this in mind as you read *My Study*.

Praise be to God.

Is Jesus God?

How could Jesus be God, if God Almighty our Father, who is Spirit, created the man, Jesus? Well now, what does the Bible teach?

In the King James Version, 1 Timothy 3:16 reads, "God was manifest in the flesh." The New World Translation uses the pronoun *He* instead of the word *God*. It makes no difference to me. John 1:1: "in the beginning was the Word" (KJV). Who was the Word in the flesh? Jesus! The real difference is to understand whose Word it *is* in the beginning. It had to be the Almighty God's, because God is the creator of all. Therefore, the Word was God!

In the King James Version, John 1:10 reads, "He was in the world and the world was made by him, and the world knew him not." This scripture is also referring to Jesus. The Bible teaches, to my understanding, that God our Father, who is Spirit, created the man, Jesus. Was He just a man? If we could check His DNA today, I think we might be very surprised at what we might find, or not find. So what do the scriptures tell us?

The first scriptures that come to mind are Isaiah 7:14 and Matthew 1:23. Isaiah reads, "Therefore the Lord Himself shall give you a sign, behold, a virgin shall conceive and bear a son, and she shall call his name Emmanuel" (KJV). Matthew reads, "behold, a virgin shall be with child, and shall bring forth a son, and they shall call his name Emmanuel, which, being interpreted, is, God with us"

(KJV). Why is the Bible being so specific about the name and its interpretation? I believe it is because of 1 Timothy 3:16, which reads, "God was manifest in the flesh" (KJV). Matthew 1:21 reads, "And she shall bring forth a son, and shall call his name Jesus" (KJV). John 1:14 reads, "And the Word was made flesh" (KJV). We know Jesus throughout the whole Bible as the Son of God, and the Word made flesh. So why would the Bible be so specific about the name *Emmanuel* and its interpretation? I believe it is to show us Jesus was God in the flesh, but how could this be?

Praise be to God.

Food for Thought

In this chapter of *My Study*, I will show you the scripture, then give you my comments and my thoughts. Remember, these are my thoughts—merely opinions. So you decide.

When we read the Bible, the Holy Word of God, we cannot look at one or two scriptures and block them in as a solid understanding. We have to look at the whole picture of what the Bible teaches in all scripture. Here's an example of what I'm saying. Matthew 14:33: "then they that were in the ship came and worshiped him, saying, of the truth thou art the Son of God" (KJV). Matthew 9:27: "and when Jesus departed thence, two blind men followed him, crying, and saying, thou son of David, have mercy on us" (KJV). Matthew 24:30: "and then shall appear the sign of the Son of man in Heaven: and then shall all the tribes of the earth mourn, and they shall see the Son of man coming in the clouds of Heaven with power and great glory" (KJV). These three versus claim Jesus to be the Son of God, the son of David, the Son of Man. Does this make Jesus three persons in one? Of course not! These are merely titles for the earthly vessel, Jesus. He is the literal Son of God. He is called the son of David, because He was born in the Jewish bloodline, in the Jewish religion. He is called the Son of Man, because He is the fleshly vessel of the Holy Spirit.

Now to take this a little further, Colossians 2:9 reads, "For in him [Jesus the fleshly man] dwelleth all the fullness of the Godhead bodily" (KJV). John 3:34 reads, "For he [Jesus the fleshly man] whom God hath sent [or created for a purpose] speaketh the Words of God: for God giveth not the Spirit by measure unto him [Jesus the fleshly man]" (KJV). So now, what do all the scriptures tell us so far? To my understanding, they are telling me that Jesus was a fleshly vessel created for the fullness of God's Spirit, which is the Holy Spirit, the Word of God. If God Almighty is creator of all, and creates with His Word, then I can truly understand why Jesus is called the Son of God, the son of David, and the Son of Man. Jesus was created to fulfill all three titles. How? Well, He was literally the created Son of God. He was literally in the bloodlines of King David, and the Jewish religion. He was literally created a man of flesh, but scripture is not literally saying He is the fleshly vessel of God Himself. But, what do the scriptures teach? John 1:14 reads, "And the Word was made flesh and dwelt among us, and we beheld his Glory, the Glory as of the only begotten of the Father full of Grace and Truth" (KJV). John 1:1 reads, "In the beginning was the Word and the Word was with God, and the Word was God" (KJV).

Now I want you to think about something. If the Word was made flesh and dwelt among us, then whose Word is it if not God the Father's? The Word was made flesh to show the Father's Glory in the person of the only begotten son. Do you see that? Jesus was the earthly vessel of God, of God the Father. This is why John 1:10 reads, "He was in the world and the world was made by him and the world knew him not" (KJV). 1 Timothy 3:16: "and without controversy great is the mystery of godliness: God was manifest in the flesh, justified in Spirit, seen of angels, preached unto the Gentiles, believed on in the world, received up into Glory"

(KJV). This, of course, is the fleshly vessel of God—Jesus the Christ.

Let's take a look at Isaiah 9:6 as well. The King James Version reads like this: "For unto us a child is born, unto us a son is given: and the government shall be upon his shoulder: and his name shall be called Wonderful, Counselor, The mighty God, The everlasting Father, The Prince of Peace." So what is this literally telling me? Jesus was the child, born into the world. Jesus was the given sacrifice for our salvation. Jesus will return and rule His creation. This is why He is called Wonderful, Counselor, The Mighty God, The Everlasting Father, The Prince of Peace. Jesus is literally God the Father. Made known to us by His flesh vessel, Jesus the Christ! What is the definition of the word *Christ*? Why of course, the Anointed One. This would mean only one thing—Jesus, the flesh man, was the Spirit and Word of God.

Now I want you to think about this, and think very deeply, please: Did Satan truly know who he was dealing with when he tempted Jesus? Luke 4:3: "And the devil said unto him, If thou be the Son of God, command this stone that it be made bread" (KJV). Luke 4:6: "And the devil said unto him, All this power will I give thee, and the glory of them: for that is delivered unto me; and to whomsoever I will, I give it" (KJV). Luke 4:9: "And he brought him to Jerusalem, and set him on a pinnacle of the Temple, and said unto him, if thou be the Son of God, cast thyself down from hence:" (KJV). Now, after reading these verses, we read Luke 4:12: "And Jesus answering said unto him, It is said, Thou shalt not tempt the Lord thy God" (KJV).

Now I want you to think about this very deeply. If Jesus was indeed the fleshly vessel of God, the Father, which I do believe this is what scripture teaches, then Satan had no idea whom he was talking to. He was speaking with his creator, and had not a clue. Why? Because he thought he was dealing only with the Son of God, a separate entity or person. Many of us may not see the whole picture in plain view, of what the scriptures actually teach. I can surely see that Satan did not get the picture—the whole picture! For if he did, he would never have tempted God Himself. Jesus, God in the fleshly vessel, told Satan face to face, ".Thou shalt not tempt the Lord thy God." But Satan heard this only as repeated scripture from a fleshly vessel. Now, realize these things: We in this world are flesh and spirit. If God made the Word flesh, which is Himself, He came into His created world as man. Then John 3:34 makes sense, because the man Jesus spoke the Words of God. Therefore, when Jesus told Satan, "Thou shalt not tempt the Lord thy God," He literally meant just that! Satan was not speaking to a second person in a trinity, or another god as the New World Translation teaches. He was literally speaking to God our Father, in all His glory-- as of-- the begotten Son, our salvation. 1 Timothy 2:3: "God our Savior!" John 14:9: "Jesus saith unto him, have I been so long time with you, and yet hast thou not known me, Philip? he that hath seen me hath seen the Father; and how sayeth thou then, show us the Father?" John 10:30: "I and my Father are one" (KJV).

Praise be to God.

Jesus, God in the Flesh

"Jesus, God in the flesh." That is quite a statement. Why? Because there is only one God. How could this mean Jesus was the second person of a Trinity, as many Christians believe? What does the Bible teach? How do the scriptures read? John 1:1 reads, "In the beginning was the Word" (KJV). Who is the Word? Jesus! Whose Word is it? The Father's Word! John 3:34 reads, "for He whom God has sent speaketh the Words of God. For God giveth not the Spirit by measure unto him" (KJV). (Remember, no Word, no God). Colossians 2:9 reads, "for in him [Jesus] dwells all the fullness of the Godhead bodily, and you are complete in him who is the head of all principality and power" (KJV). Sounds like Almighty to me. And Colossians 2:9–10 reads like this: "Because it is in him [Jesus] that all the fullness of the divine quality dwells bodily and so you are possessed of a fullness by means of him who is the head of all government and authority" (NWT). It is my understanding, by this scripture alone, that Jesus contains the fullness in Spirit of God Jehovah, our Father in Heaven. Now when I say fullness, as the scriptures read, I mean just that! So, if Jesus contains the fullness of God in Spirit, and has all the power and authority given unto Him, as the only anointed earthly vessel created, does this make Him God in the flesh? Well now, what do the scriptures teach? Remember John 1:1: "In the beginning was the Word and the Word was with God, and the Word was God" (KJV). How could the Word be a god when Deuteronomy 32:39 says, "there is no god with me:" (KJV). How could Jesus be the second person of a trinity, a separate entity, when Isaiah 45:5 reads, "I am the Lord, and there is none else, there is no God beside me:" (KJV). I can clearly understand through scripture that Jesus was God in an anointed flesh vessel, but not as a second person of a trinity, a separate entity. Why would I think this? In the King James Version, Isaiah 45:5 states, "There is no God beside me." Notice that the *G* in the word *God* is a capital *G*. This may seem to be confusing or a contradiction, because we know the scripture tells us that Jesus sits at the right hand of the Father. If we see Jesus as a separate entity, or second person of a Trinity, as God the Son, how then can the scripture read, "There is no God beside me"?

One very important word in the scripture in John 1:1 in both the King James Version and the New World Translation is the word *with*. And it is not important just in these few scriptures I mention now, but in all scripture in the entire text of each Bible. The Bible teaches me that the word *with* is not to be understood as "alongside of"; rather it is to be understood as it appears in 1 Corinthians 15:28 (KJV)—all in all! Philippians 2:6 reads, "being in the form of God, though it not robbery to be equal with God" (KJV). What are the scriptures teaching? Let's take it one step at a time. The body of Jesus, or vessel—that which contains the fullness in Spirit of God the Father—acted upon His will always as the Father instructed. Why? Because Jesus showed complete understanding of who the Father is. Why? Because God our Father wanted the world to know who He is. John 17:25: "oh righteous Father, the world have not known thee: but I have known thee, and these have known that thou hast sent me" (KJV). When Jesus says, "these have known that thou hast sent me," He is speaking of His disciples.

I see it like this. Jesus, the fleshly man, born in the world, known in the world as the son of Mary and Joseph, was seen by the people around Him as a natural man. If we would have been born at that time, and knew the family history of Jesus, we would have looked at Him as one of us, a human being. Of course He was a human being. But, do you want to check His DNA? Number one, Joseph was His earthly father, "as was supposed," according to Luke 3:23 (KJV). This is exactly how the scripture reads—"as was supposed." Jesus, born of the flesh, was adopted into the bloodline of Joseph in the Jewish faith. Number two, Jesus, our mediator for spiritual adoption, was the Son of God, or the fleshly vessel that contained the fullness of Spirit, of God Jehovah, our Father in Heaven, as the Bible teaches, the Word made flesh. The world didn't know this. The world around Him, or the people who knew Him, saw only a man. We must keep this in mind as we read all scripture pertaining to Jesus, the Son of God. Jesus, the man of flesh filled with the Spirit of God, was adopted into the family of flesh. We, as Christians through Christ Jesus, are adopted into the spiritual family of God Jehovah, our Father in Heaven.

This would mean, by all scriptures in each translations, that the word *with* means together as one. To see and understand this is, think of blue *with* yellow, which is green! All in all, as one! To fully comprehend my example, you must get out your Bible and your pen and pad. Write down how you disagree with me. Then continue reading *My Study*. You may disagree; this is your God-given right. But please, get out of your box, and seek Him diligently. Your box consists of the four walls of doctrine that make up your religious beliefs. If you read *My Study*, you may see and understand by scripture and only scripture, that there is no trinity and no two Gods, one with a capital *G* and one with a lower case *g*, as the New World Translation teaches. God is Almighty! Almighty God! Do you understand this? This means there is no other, and the Word was *God*!

If you were God Almighty, invisible Spirit, how would you show humankind who you truly are? Jesus quoted in John 18:37, "I should bear witness unto the truth."

Praise be to God.

Led by the Spirit

Okay, we know Jesus was flesh—a man—or, you might say, the perfect anointed vessel containing the fullness in Spirit of God Jehovah, our Father. John 3:34: "for he whom God hath sent [or created] speaketh the Words of God: for God giveth not the Spirit by measure unto him" (KJV). I believe Jesus was created by the Almighty invisible Spirit of God for this purpose. Colossians 2:9 of the King James Version reads, "for in him dwelleth all the fullness of the Godhead bodily" (KJV). The key word here is *bodily*. I believe the scripture means just that. The fullness of God's Spirit was in that body, or the anointed vessel of Jesus. Colossians 2:9 of the New World Translation reads, "because it is in him that all the fullness of the divine quality dwells bodily." I believe that the New World Translation is stating the same knowledge as the King James Version. I believe both Bibles are speaking of the body, or anointed vessel of Jesus!

So you might ask, why would God Almighty put His fullness of Spirit in His Son? First of all, let me express some of my deepest thoughts in my understanding of the Bible and what it teaches. A question was asked of me long ago: "If God can do anything, could He create something so heavy that He could not lift it?" My answer was, "Of course. God can do anything." The reply was, "Well, He can't do anything if He can't lift what He created that was so heavy." At the time I didn't feel as if I truly knew the answer. But now, after studying scripture, I truly know God can do whatever He wills.

Think about this! God created man and gave him a free will. The definition of free will is the ability to make a choice after fully judging the circumstances. The one choice man may consider is the love of God, or the love of the world. It was God Almighty who created the world and everything in it. God gave man free will because of His love, which He expected to receive in return. God so loved the world that He gave His only [anointed earthly vessel, or] begotten son." (John 3:16 KJV). Man's free will, more often than not, leads to sin, and sin will lead to death. This is the heavy object that God created that He cannot lift.

God wanted man to love and trust in Him by a free will, not by force. But God our Father did not want any to perish. So He found a way, we might say, to lift this heavy object. It was Jesus. You might say, but that's not God doing the lifting. Well, as I see it, God is the creator of all, and it was His doing, His will, His creation. So it seems to me it would be His responsibility for man's salvation. 1 Timothy 2:3 reads, "For this is good and acceptable insight of God our Savior" (NKJV). Who is the Savior of the world? Jesus, of course! 1 Timothy 2:4 reads, "Who will have all men to be saved, and to come unto the knowledge of the truth" (KJV). Keep in mind that *truth* is the key word. 1 Timothy 2:5 reads, "For there is one God, and one mediator between God and men, the man Christ Jesus;" (KJV). Keep in mind the word *man*, as Christ was flesh. 1 Timothy 2:6 reads, "who gave himself a ransom for all, to be testified in due time" (KJV). Keep in mind the words *due time*, for the flesh will reveal the spirit it contains.

Let's look at this next scripture closely. 1 Timothy 4:10 reads, "For therefore we both labor and suffer reproach, because we trust in the living God, who is the saviour of all men, specially of those that believe" (KJV). When Paul wrote to Timothy about the living God "who is the Savior of all men," I believe he was referring to Jesus, even though Paul had never known Jesus in the flesh. Before Paul was called by Jesus to preach His Word, Jesus was already in Heaven, as one with the Father.

But Paul did live, walk, and preach with men who had seen and known Jesus in the flesh. They were still alive and preaching God's Word when Paul came to be a part of God's Word by preaching the Church-Age, or Grace-Age gospel. So I believe that Paul, knowing Jesus and His Word, was referring to the Spirit of God our Father that dwelled in the living body of Jesus and now lives in Heaven. He is the Savior of all men.

Jesus said, in Revelations 1:8, "I am Alpha and Omega, the beginning and the ending" (KJV). How could Jesus say this? Go back to John1:1: "the Word was God" (KJV). So, if Jesus was a living anointed vessel, filled with God's Spirit, and always led by the Spirit of God our Father, He is the Almighty Spirit of God in an anointed fleshly vessel; in other words, He is God in the flesh. Why and how do we truly know this? Let's look at this scripture very closely. John 1:18 reads, "no man hath seen God at any time; the only begotten son, which is in the bosom of the Father, he hath declared him" (KJV). What is flesh? It is a container, or vessel only. What is Spirit? It is the true nature, or foundation, of reality, of expression released by that vessel, or body. So what is John

1:18 saying? The word *declare*, as I understand it, means to make known clearly. Also the word *bosom* is defined as such: intimate or confidential. The word *intimate* is defined as innermost, or deep within, as an intimate friend or associate. The word *confidence* indicates confidence or intimacy, and could describe one entrusted with private affairs, or a person to whom secrets are confided.

Okay, having a better understanding of the word *knowledge*, I see John 1:18 reading as plain as this: No man has seen God at any time. In this, John is only making a true statement of fact. But, then he says, "the only begotten son." He is, of course, referring to Jesus. But then he says, "which is in the bosom of the Father." Now having a better understanding of the word *bosom*, I can't help but to go back to John 1:1: "In the beginning was the Word and the Word was with God, and the Word was God" (KJV). The last line of John 1:18 is the most important to understand: "He hath declared Him." Knowing Jesus was an anointed vessel sent by God our Father, filled with His fullness of Spirit, as described in Colossians 2:9, I can truly understand the last line of this scripture of John 1:18. This scripture plainly tells me that God, the Almighty invisible Spirit, created the anointed vessel Jesus, the only begotten son, of whom He is well pleased, so that God could come to His creation, as His creation, for the salvation of humankind. This would be the only way humankind could intimately know the Almighty invisible Spirit, God Jehovah, our Father in Heaven.

Jesus, being filled with His Divine Spirit, was always led by His Spirit. Why?

- To lift that heavy object, which is sin.
- To teach us the knowledge and wisdom of God our Father.
- To teach us the character of God our Father.
- To show us the love and mercy of God our Father.
- To open our eyes and hearts to God our Father's Word.
- To give possible light in the darkness of this world. The light is to understand God's Word. The darkness is not knowing God our Father, and to live and die in blind sin.
- To teach us, by Jesus's complete actions, who God our Father is. Jesus lived in the flesh among men. He was seen from the eyes of men.
- To teach us about the present and the future, and give us understanding of the past.

Jesus lived with us so that we could see the hope of our salvation by His shed blood, His unmerciful torment, the ultimate of pain and suffering, the embarrassment of a righteous man being condemned of sin, and the pain of a broken heart because of the actions of humankind. Jesus, who was all love, filled with the Spirit of love, which is God our Father, said these words in Luke 23:34 "Father, forgive them; for they know not what they do" (KJV). Jesus, even at the cross, in all His pain and betrayal by humankind, still taught us the love of the Father.

I believe that, by the life of Jesus on this planet, Jesus declared Him, the Father, by letting the Father be known to us in all clarity. So Jesus, being an anointed vessel, or body filled with the fullness of God our Father, had all the vitals of God, which are, love, truth, righteousness, wisdom, and all authority and power. Who do you say He is? Remember that the body is only a container for the spirit. This body dies and rots away, but the spirit lives on. We will be resurrected in a new spiritual vessel for eternal life, a spiritual body, and Spirit as one in Christ, as Christ is one in the Father.

Praise be to God.

In the Name of Jesus

As Christians, we all pray to the Father in the name of Jesus. I believe we pray in the name of Jesus for many reasons, but the most evident by the scripture is to claim the one and only true God. There are many religions throughout the world. In various religions, humankind worships a God or gods as a higher being or beings, as creator or creators of all. Some religions may have more than one god. The world is full of religions and many gods. If we were to speak about God anywhere in the world and just use the word *God*, chances are people would not be offended. Sad to say, even in this country, if one speaks of God, most everyone is at ease, but if we use the name Jesus, some people may start to feel uneasy. Why would the name Jesus make a person feel uneasy? I believe it is because Jesus is the name above all names. How can I say this? What do the scriptures tell us?

John 10:25 in the King James Version reads, "I told you, and ye believed not: the works that I do in my Father's name, they bear witness of me." I know the name of Jesus is not a name we call the Father. Almighty God our Father had many names, or titles, in the Old Testament. Jesus taught us to pray and ask of all things to our Father, as He did always. Now, in the scripture, Jesus said, "the works that I do in my Father's name, they bear witness of me." Okay. Remember that Jesus, the anointed man of flesh, is a container filled with the fullness of Jehovah God, our Father in Spirit. So when He said, "in my Father's name, they bear witness of me," He is saying the Almighty, powerful God Jehovah, our Father's Spirit, is at work in the world through Him: "is a witness of me"—Jesus! Now when Jesus says, "bear witness of me," He is actually saying that the works are a testimony of evidence of who He is. Who was He? John 10:30 in the King James Version reads, "I and my Father are one." I know what you might be thinking. If Jesus was flesh, and always prayed to the Father, how could they be one, except that Jesus was His son? Yes, He is the Son of God, a vessel created by the Almighty invisible Spirit, an anointed vessel that contained the fullness of that Almighty Spirit, as the next scripture confirms. Colossians 2:9, in the New World Translation reads, "because it is in him that all the fullness of the divine quality dwells bodily." Also remember John 3:34 in the King James Version—Jesus contained that Spirit with no measure. This would confirm only one thing: they are one in Spirit completely, in the completion of His Word, in the everlasting dispensation of time, by the foreknowledge of God, before the world was, *is*, and is to come. The alpha and omega.

John 10:37 of the King James Version reads, "if I do not the works of my Father, believe me not." Look at what Jesus is saying here, but first remember, Jesus is seen and heard only as a man of flesh. The flesh in all humankind has the nature of sin, so when Jesus said, "If I do not the works of my Father, believe me not," He means "Okay, you believe I'm just a man with a sinful nature, as you are. If I were a sinner, then, of course, don't believe me."

In the next scripture John 10:38 (KJV), my opinion is Jesus is saying, "But if I do my Father's will, and you still don't believe me (me as a fleshly man), then at least believe the works of My Father—not the works of me (the fleshly man), but of me as Spirit, as one with my Father."

Okay, I'm going to write the next two scriptures. I want you to read them and determine for yourself what the King James Version scriptures mean. John 10:38 reads, "but if I do, though ye believe not me, believe the works: that ye may know, and believe, that the Father is in me, and I in him." Colossians 3:17 reads, "And whatsoever ye do in word or deed, do all in the name of the Lord Jesus, giving thanks to God and the Father by him" (KJV).

Well, there it is—they are as one in Spirit. Keep that in mind that Jesus is our Savior. 1 Timothy 2:3: "God our Savior" (NKJV). So why should we pray to the Father in the name of Jesus?

- Jesus was a living body; in all His teaching and actions during His life he showed, and expressed to us in all nature, who the Father is.
- Why would He do this? Because He is the Word of God—not a messenger of the Word. John the Baptist preached the coming Messiah, the Word of God. John 3:34 of the King James Version reads: "For he whom God hath sent speaketh the words of God: for God giveth not the Spirit by measure unto him". Jesus was the Word made flesh. 1 Timothy 3:16 in any Christian Bible tells us this. But, the King James Version reads, "God was manifest in the flesh." This, of course is correct. God, the Almighty invisible Spirit was filled in that anointed fleshly

vessel, known to us as Jesus the created fleshly vessel, the Son of God.

- Jesus the man of flesh, died for our sins, but whose will was it? And who created Him for that purpose? It was God Almighty, our Father, our Savior (1 Timothy 2:3: "God our Savior" (NKJV).
- Remember, Almighty Jehovah God, our Father, is Spirit. John 4:24 and Colossians 1:15—the invisible God (KJV). He always was and will be. So, if He always was, and the Word was in the beginning, as John 1:1 states, in the King James Version, the Word always, of course, was His, God Almighty's. So the Almighty Spirit made the Word flesh so that the world could know Him intimately, as He desired, and not just as a greater being of all creation, but as our Father of all creation. He gave us a way to be born again through Jesus Christ—to be born of His Spirit and claimed as one of His, and not of this world, but one Spirit with Him.

So why is the name of Jesus so important?

- He is the Son of God, the Word made flesh (1 Timothy 3:16), the Word, God Almighty, Jehovah God, our Father in Heaven.
- He is our Savior, the only way—by adoption—into the family of God our Father.
- By the life of Jesus, we come to know our eternal Father, the one and true God. John 17: 3 in the King James Version reads, "And this is life eternal, that they might know thee the only true God, and Jesus Christ, whom thou hast sent." When we read

in the scripture, "and Jesus Christ, whom thou hast sent." Remember, Jesus was the anointed earthly vessel of the Almighty invisible Spirit. You cannot separate body and spirit on this planet. They were one in the same!

Praise be to God.

What about a Trinity?

I believe and know there is only one God. How can I say this? The Holy Bible. I believe the scriptures are very clear. Anyone who reads the scriptures will see the face value of each scripture. If the scripture sounds like a contradiction, you will learn by other scripture how at first it may look this way. If you read the books of the Bible and keep in mind that there is only one God, and He is Spirit (John 4:24), then the scriptures will all make sense.

When I am reading scripture, I always keep in mind that there is only one God. Deuteronomy 32:39 reads, "see now that I, even I am he, and there is no god with me:" (KJV). Isaiah 45:5 reads, "I am the Lord, and there is no other; there is no God beside me" (KJV).

Another scripture that is always in my mind is John 1:1: "in the beginning was the Word, and the Word was with God, and the Word was God" (KJV). This scripture is so very important to understand. Think about the scriptures! If God Almighty always was, surely, long before the beginning, as in always, the Word was God, as God, in all power and authority. Which means the Word is God. But the scripture reads, "In the beginning was the Word, and the Word was with God, and the Word was God." Well now, if this scripture is talking about the creation of the world as the beginning, then of course it would have had to be God Almighty who spoke it into existence, because He is the Almighty, the creator of all.

But, what does John 1:3 say? It reads, "All things were made by him; and without him was not anything made that was made" (KJV). Now, after reading the first chapter of the Gospel according to John, I'm sure we can all agree that John 1:3 refers to Jesus. Why? Because He is known as the anointed flesh vessel, which contained the fullness of God, in Spirit, known as the Word of God. Why would He be known as the Word of God? Because the fleshly man Jesus was literally the Spiritual Word of God. (First Timothy 3:16: "the Word made flesh."). The King James Version states that *God* was manifest in the flesh. The New World Translation states that *He* was manifest in flesh. This scripture does differ, but I understand them both as the same. How can I say this? God Almighty is the creator of all. He spoke everything into existence with His Word. John 1:10 in the King James Version reads, "He was in the world, and the world was made by him, and the world knew him not." Now, as you can hopefully see, this scripture also refers to Jesus. The King James Version says in this scripture that the world was made by Him, meaning Jesus. The New World Translation reads, "He was in the world and the world came into existence through him, but the world did not know him." Okay, these two scriptures do differ by word choice in translation. The King James Versions states "made by him." The New World Translation states "came into existence through him." One might say that the difference in word choice can cause a great misunderstanding of the content. I don't think so! I see both scriptures—the King James Version and the New World Translation—telling me the same thing; that is, God Almighty created the world. How can I say this? If both scriptures are referring to Jesus, simply read the first book of Genesis. God Almighty created the world. Read 1 Timothy 3:16 in the King James Version: "God manifest in the flesh." Read Colossians 2:9–10 in the New World Translation: "because it is in him, that all the fullness of the divine quality dwells bodily." Also in the New World Translation, read Deuteronomy 32:39: "see now that I, I am he, and there is no gods together with me." Also in the New World Translation, read Isaiah 45:18: "I am Jehovah, and there is no one else." Well then, how could the created Son of God be the creator of all? Simple—the anointed fleshly vessel in the world, Jesus, was the Almighty Spirit of God Jehovah, our Father in Heaven. His Spirit as Jesus was sent to a sinful and dying world. This, of course, was for an intimate knowledge of God, and salvation.

Now I want you to picture this in your mind: God Almighty, as invisible Spirit, who is in you and in me, and everywhere at once, is sitting on His throne. He is looking down at His creation. He sees His Son, Jesus, doing His most important work, showing the world who God is, then giving His life for us. Or, is Jesus showing the world who He is (Jesus), as a separate entity, or another god? Also what about the Holy Spirit that works within us? The point is this: if Jesus and the Holy Spirit are separate entities of a trinity, or another god as the New World Translation insinuates, what then? The fleshly man Jesus in this world was the Word of God. The Word is all power and authority. From all the love within creation, Jesus gave His life for us. If he was not literally God Almighty in an anointed fleshly vessel, known as the Son of God, what then? Is the Almighty God of Heaven sitting on His throne under a sign raised high above His head that reads, "I am the Almighty God"? *I think not!* It was God our Father who did it all! Because He is, all in all, Almighty God!

So what am I saying? God Almighty, our Father, is Spirit. John 4:24 in any Christian bible tells us this. Jesus says in John 3:8 in the King James Version, "the Spirit is like the wind. You know not where it comes from." What I believe Jesus means by "like the wind" is that you cannot see Spirit, but because of the wind, you can see movement of the trees, bushes, and other things. As so, because of the Spirit, you can see the fruits it bears, or the actions of the Spirit. We cannot see God our Father as Spirit, but we can know and feel His love. We can see His actions through the life of Jesus Christ. Remember that the body is merely a container for the Spirit. Jesus was His only begotten son, an anointed created vessel for the Spirit of God, Jehovah, our Father, our Savior. Through Jesus Christ all things are known to us even now. How? Through His Holy Spirit. And who is the Holy Spirit? God, the One and Only. John 4:24!

Well now, here is the Holy Spirit. Remember the Bible says that Jesus sits at the right hand of the Father? And I said that perhaps the Holy Spirit is at His left hand. Well I really don't think so. This is what I truly believe: Jesus was created by God Almighty our Father. He was born of a virgin here on Earth, filled with the Holy Spirit in His mother's womb, and born for the purpose of our salvation and to give us complete knowledge of our Father in Heaven. Jesus, of course, was flesh, but His Holy Spirit was of God. The Spirit He was born with was His Spirit, our Father God Almighty's.

As Jesus grew and came to the time of His baptism, He had long preached His Father's Word. The scripture says that, when Jesus (the anointed fleshly vessel) was baptized, the Holy Spirit ascended on Him like a dove. It was only after His baptism that Jesus performed His first miracle. This tells me something. I believe at this time Almighty God our Father gave Jesus complete authority to act upon His Word. Jesus is known as the Word of God. Why? To preach, to show, and to act upon the Word of God.

The Bible teaches that Jesus was, in the beginning, with the Father, and I know He was—in Spirit, the Holy Spirit, the Spirit of God Almighty, our Father. How do I know this? John 1:1 in the King James Version reads, "in the beginning was the Word, and the Word was with God, and the Word was God." I believe Jesus was born with the Holy Spirit. But I believe it was at His baptism, when the dove ascended on Him, that He was anointed with the fullness of God Almighty to act upon His Word with all power and authority. Jesus then became a living witness of God in the flesh. He performed no miracles before the Spirit ascended on Him, yet He was born with the Holy Spirit of God.

You might ask, how can I say all this? Well, here it is! Matthew 1:20 reads, "but while he thought on these things, behold, the angel of the Lord appeared unto him in a dream, saying, Joseph thou son of David, fear not to take on to thee Mary thy wife; for that which is conceived in her is of the Holy Ghost [or Spirit]" (KJV). Note, when it says "of the Holy Spirit," this does not mean from God; rather, it means "in fullness," as taught by scripture. How can I say this? Matthew 1:23 in the King James Version reads,

"Behold, a virgin shall be with child, and shall bring forth a son, and they shall call his name Emmanuel, which, being interpreted, is, God with us." This is also in reference to 1 Timothy 3:16 in the King James Version: "God manifest in the flesh."

In reference to John the Baptist, Luke 1:15 in the King James Version reads, "For he shall be great in the sight of the Lord, and shall drink neither wine nor strong drink; and he shall be filled with the Holy Ghost [or spirit], even from his mother's womb." If John the Baptist was filled with the Holy Spirit from his mother's womb, then of course Jesus would be. And, of course, Jesus, unlike John at his baptism, was anointed with all power and authority to be the living Word of God in this world.

John 20:21–22 in the King James Version reads, "Then said Jesus to them again, peace be unto you: as my Father has sent me, even so send I you. And when he had said this, he breathed on them, and saith unto them, Receive ye the Holy Ghost:" This, to my understanding, would be to receive understanding of His Word, the power of His Word, and, of course, salvation.

John 20:21–22 in the New World Translation reads like this: Jesus, therefore, said to them again: "May you have peace. Just as the Father has sent me forth, I also am sending you." And after he said this he blew upon them and said to them: "Receive Holy Spirit."

These two verses tell me the same thing; that is, through Jesus Christ our Savior, we can come to know our Father in

Heaven. So where is the Holy Spirit? He is in the hearts of all believers here on planet Earth—the Spirit of the Righteous One, the Holy One, the Anointed One, Jesus. His Spirit will separate us from the spirit of this world, and lead us to the family of God our Father in Heaven. When we come to know Jesus as Lord and Savior, we will receive His Spirit, the Holy Spirit of Almighty God, our adoption!

How can I say this? Acts 2:38: "then Peter said unto them, repent and be baptized every one of you in the name of Jesus Christ for the remission of sins, and you shall receive the gift of the Holy Ghost. For the promises is unto you and to your children, and to all that are afar off, even as many as the Lord our God shall call" (KJV). I believe this scripture is describing a baptism of the Holy Spirit—not a water baptism, but a true baptism of His Spirit. This, of course, would be salvation, for by His Spirit, we received Grace, and we are saved. It is our choice, and it is free.

Well, there it is. One God, one Spirit, one Salvation. John 4:24: "God is Spirit, and they that worship him must worship him in Spirit and in Truth" (KJV). Matthew 1:23: "behold, a virgin shall be with child, and shall bring forth a son, and they shall call his name Emmanuel, which, being interpreted, is, God with us." (KJV). John 20:22: "Receive the Holy Spirit" (NKJV)

Note: in the first scripture of John, he is telling us God is Spirit. This, of course, would be the Almighty Holy Spirit. In the scripture of Matthew, the Bible is specifically saying God is with us. This, of course, is the newborn child, Jesus the Christ. I see the second scripture of John telling me that, if we believe in Jesus Christ as Lord and Savior, we will receive His Spirit. His Spirit, of course, is of the Almighty God our Father in Heaven. So I see only one God, one Spirit, and one Salvation, Jesus the Christ. Isaiah 9:6 tells me this is so. As the scripture reads from the King James Version: "For unto us a child is born, unto us a son is given, and the government shall be upon his shoulder; and his name shall be called Wonderful, Counselor, The mighty God, The everlasting Father, The Prince of peace." This scripture alone tells me there are not three individual entities that equal one God, as a trinity. This scripture, as well as many others in the Bible, convinces me that there is only one God, one Spirit, one Salvation. He, of course, is God Almighty. All in all.

Praise be to God.

Jesus Returns to Heaven

Hebrews 10:12: "But this man, after he had offered one sacrifice for sins forever, sat down on the right hand of God;" (KJV).

Hebrews 12:2: "looking unto Jesus the author and finisher of our faith; who for the joy that was set before him endured the cross, despising the shame, and is set down at the right hand of the throne of God" (KJV.)

Ephesians 1:20: "Which he had wrought [or worked] in Christ, when he raised him from the dead, and set him at his own right hand in the Heavenly places," (KJV).

Colossians 3:1: "If ye then be risen with Christ, seek those things which are above, where Christ sitteth on the right hand of God" (KJV).

First Corinthians 15:28: "and when all things shall be subdued unto him, then shall the son also himself be subject unto him that put all things under him, that God may be all in all" (KJV).

First Corinthians 15:28: "But when all things are subjected to Him, then the son Himself also will be subjected to the One who has subjected all things to Him, that God may be all things in all." (Interlinear Bible Hebrew-Greek-English).

Now, as I understand scripture, the Spirit of God always was. That Spirit in action is His Word. He created the world and the Heavens by actions of His Word. His Word is the existence of being. His Word is truth, it is just, it is all knowledge, power, and authority. The Word is God Almighty. The Word would be the complete foundation of God Almighty. How can I say this? No Word, no God. Think about what the scriptures teach us. It tells us, in all my understanding, that the Word of God spoken is the action of His Spirit, and the fruit it will bear. God creates by His Spirit, which is His Word.

Now when I say the Word of God, I'm not just thinking of the Bible, or of Jesus Christ. I am thinking of the creator, of God Almighty, the creator of all. His Word is all power in knowledge and truth of His very existence. Knowing this, I can see why He sent or created Jesus Christ, the anointed vessel, filled with His Spirit. Through Christ we can know God our Father. Jesus was the living Word in the world. By the life of Jesus in all truth and actions of His life here on Earth, we can see and know our Father through Him, God's anointed fleshly vessel. How can I say this? Jesus was the living Spirit of God our Father in the world as flesh. Jesus said it Himself: John 14:9 "Have I been so long time with you, and yet hast thou not known me, Philip? He that hast seen me hast seen the Father; and how sayest thou then, Shew us the Father?" (KJV). John 10:30 "I and my Father are one" (KJV). (And they are, in Spirit.) This is why John 1:1 is so very powerful in truth: "In the beginning was the Word, and the Word was with God, and the Word was God" (KJV). With this scripture alone, I can say there is only one God. Yet I can see and understand the Godhead, or so-called trinity as Father, as Son, and Holy Spirit, or as the Bible puts it, the Word of God:

- The Father as the Word.
- The Son created by the Word, to be filled with the living Word as a witness on Earth, of the Word.
- The Spirit of that creation, of that living Word, by the Word of God our Father, who now lives in us through the hearing of the Word.
- Jesus Christ, the Son of God, yet the Spirit of God in fullness.

The fact that Jesus came in the fullness of the Spirit of God is what makes Him God in the flesh. The body is nothing but a container. Your spirit is your true identity. The identity of Jesus Christ is the Holy Spirit, God Almighty!

We as believers have received a gift of His Spirit. When we as believers go to be with the Father in Heaven, then we will be in union with the Father, as one in Spirit. How can I say this? Jesus Christ, who has given us the Word of God, has made us free of sin. A person must be perfect to enter into Heaven. No one is perfect without the blood of Christ. But, as believers, we are perfect in the sight of God our Father. Only then may we enter into Heaven with Christ as one Spirit, in union with God our Father.

So when we read that Jesus sits at the right hand of God, is this a literal statement? I am confused, but if it is spiritually speaking, I can understand it fully. Why and how? One Word, one Spirit, one God! The word *sit* refers to the word *seat*. This word is defined as to occupy with authority. The word *right* refers to everything just, all truth, all righteousness. The word *hand* refers to a helper. Jesus occupies all of these qualities. Jesus is in Heaven as one with the Father. He was created by the Word to be the Word, and now He is the eternal Word—all in all. The Bible says Jesus is King of Kings and Lord of Lords. He is the Alpha and Omega, the beginning and the end. Think about what the scriptures are saying. If Jesus is the beginning and the end, then and only then does John 1:1 in the King James Version make any sense. It reads, "In the beginning was the Word, the Word was with God, and the Word was God." Note: this means all in all, or as one Spirit. This scripture simply tells me that Jesus is the eternal existing Spirit of God Almighty. The Bible teaches us that God knew us long before the creation of the world. Knowing this truth, I can understand the spiritual existence of Jesus, long before His birth on planet Earth.

I believe that, in the womb, and at birth, the fleshly body, or anointed vessel, of Jesus contained the fullness in Spirit of God, the creator of all. The body is not who we truly are. We are the spirit that the body contains. This is who we truly are.

We are not born in this world with the fullness of God's Spirit as Jesus was, but if we will it from God, we will receive the gift of that Spirit through Jesus Christ. That is how we receive the gift of the Holy Spirit. This is to know we have become as one with Christ Jesus in the family of God our Father. This is the gift of Grace, through Jesus Christ. We are made a righteous Spirit. Only then can we enter into Heaven. The Spirit of Jesus was always there, but through Him our Spirit is also there. God our Father was never alone! This, of course, was known to God our Father before the foundation of the world. This is why the Bible reads, "let us make man [create man] in our image." God knew who would come to Him, as one in Spirit with the Alpha and Omega, the beginning and the end, the eternal and everlasting Father, God Almighty. Jesus sits at the right hand of God in Spirit, totally united as one in Spirit always and forever. Remember, Jesus is the Son of God our Father in creation of physical being, but also remember that being in Spirit is 100 percent God Almighty as He sits on His throne.

Jesus was the Lamb of God; he paid the price for all sin. Now He is the judge, the King of kings, the Lord of Lords. There is no name above His in Heaven, or on Earth. (Get that, please—in Heaven or on Earth!)

Well, how can I say all this? Again, this scripture comes to mind: Isaiah 9:6, which reads, "For unto us a child is born, unto us a son is given; and the government shall be upon his shoulder: and his name shall be called Wonderful, Counsellor, The mighty God, The everlasting Father, The Prince of peace" (KJV). This scripture states that the government shall be upon the shoulders of Jesus. If this is truth, as I know it is, this means that Jesus will govern over all. So let's look at what the Webster's New World Dictionary has to say about the word *govern*. It means to rule by right of authority, "1 to exercise authority over, rule, control, ect. 2 to influence the action of; guide. 3 to determine". Well, I would have to say this means Jesus is King of kings and Lord of lords. We know Jesus will reign in His everlasting kingdom on Earth, but what we might fail to realize is that the kingdom on Earth is as it is in Heaven. So now, is Jesus God Almighty? What do the scriptures teach?

Praise be to God.

Jesus Sits at the Right Hand of God

Well now, how can we comprehend this if there is only One God, as the King James Version reads in Deuteronomy 32:39 states, "see now that I, even I, am he, and there is no god with me." Isaiah 45:5: "I am the Lord, and there is no other; There is no God beside me" (KJV).

Okay, that is cut and dried. We can surely see the Bible teaches only one God. I do heartily agree and understand. There can only be one God, and He is Almighty God. This means God needs no help outside of His own power and wisdom to create or to accomplish anything. He is God Almighty. Look at the words of Isaiah 45:5–8 of the King James Version:

> (5) "I am the Lord, and there is none else, there is (no God beside me:) I girded thee, though thou hast not known me: (6) That they may know from the rising of the sun and from the West, that there (is none beside me.) I am the Lord, and there is none else. (7) I form the light, and create darkness: I make peace, and create evil: I the Lord do all these things. (8) Drop-down, ye Heavens, from above, and let the skies pour down righteousness: let the earth open, and let righteousness spring up together; I the Lord have created it."

Let's also take a look at Isaiah 45:18: "For thus saith the Lord that created the Heavens; God himself that formed the earth and made it; he hath established it, he created it not in vain, he formed it to be inhabited: I am the Lord; and there (is none else)" (KJV). Now, by the Word of God, I can surely see and know there is only one God, and He is Almighty. Also, verses 5, "there is no God beside me" (KJV). This, of course, would eliminate Jesus as a god (with a lower case *g*). It also eliminates the thought of a three-person or three-entity Godhead. This, of course, is taught as a trinity to most Christian believers, mainly because the Bible does state that Jesus sits at the right hand of God. This, spiritually, is to be understood by all scripture. Also notice in verse five, the word *God* is capitalized. This is plainly telling me there is only one God, one Spirit, one Salvation!

If we are following a religion that teaches a trinity, we must understand the Word of God and the reason it may be taught. If it is taught that there is only one God, and He is Almighty, then how can three gods equal one Almighty God? How then can the New World Translation teach two gods—one with a lower case *g* as the Word, and one with a capital *G* as the Almighty God Jehovah. In my understanding of scripture, with the knowledge from many Bible translations, it is my conclusion that there is only one Almighty God. To my understanding of scripture, the word *with* as used in scripture ("the Word was with God") is used to show us that He is all in all. Whether we use the word *besides* or *beside* in scripture truly makes no difference. Why? Both understandings of the words imply that there is only one God, and He is Almighty God. There could be no other in any shape or form. "My Father said, I am He, and there is no other." Why? He is All Mighty God!

So what does the Bible mean, or the Word of God mean, when we read Genesis 1:1–25? These verses state how God Almighty, or our Father in Heaven, alone, by Himself, created the Heavens and the Earth, and everything in it, in any Christian bible. But Genesis 1:26 reads, "And God said, let us make man in our image, after our likeness" (KJV). This sounds like some great contradiction. Let us go to the book of John 1:10: "He was in the world, and the world was made by Him, and the world knew Him not" (KJV). Okay, this scripture is clearly speaking of Jesus. This scripture, as well as many more, implies that Jesus, the created Son of God Almighty, is the creator of all. You might say, how can this be? Is the Bible in contradiction? No it is not! We must read and understand what we read. All scriptures can be clearly understood with regard to the dispensation in time of its content. We must remember what we have learned from the Holy scriptures. Number one! When we read John 1:1, we must realize whose Word it is. It is God Almighty's Word. How can I say this? No Word, no God! If God is Almighty, surely it is His Word. When we read, "and the Word was with God," are we to understand that Jesus was next to God in the beginning? Or does the word *with* mean "together as one." Because "the Word was God," as it reads (KJV). Here are two examples of how the word *with* can be used and understood: I went with a friend to the store. If you mix blue with yellow, as *one*, you have the color green. The word *with* can mean together as one, as blue with yellow is green.

Now, we must remember that all things were known to God before the foundation of the world. If God knew you, me, and everyone else before the foundation of the world, then I can clearly understand why the Bible states, "let us make man in our image." All things are known to God from start to finish, before they ever exist. So when we read scripture concerning the Godhead, the Father, the created Son of God, or the Holy Spirit, remember that all of what we learn was known to God before the teaching Word of scripture ever existed. It was always in God's knowledge. So when we read, "let us make man in our image," or we learn that Jesus, the created Son of God, created the world and was in the world, this is to let us understand how the one-and-only God, Son, and Spirit dwells in all of us who believe the Word of God Almighty, our Father in Heaven. We are one in Christ, as Christ is one in the Father. Remember, there are many members in the body of Christ. We, as created man, of the natural birth, through Christ Jesus, are made in the image of God. One Spirit! I will try to explain it, scripture after scripture, as I understand it.

- John 1:1: "In the beginning was the Word and the Word was with God, and the Word was God" (KJV).
- 1 Timothy 3:16: "God was manifest in the flesh" (KJV). Why was He manifest in the flesh? So we could know the Father intimately, through His anointed created vessel, Jesus, and to shed His (God our Father's) created blood for the salvation of those who believe in God's Almighty Word. This would be the Christ!

- Matthew 1:23: "Behold, a virgin shall be with child, and shall bring forth a son, and they shall call his name Emmanuel, which being interpreted is, God with us" (KJV). The word *they* in this scripture refers to the people of this world. The Bible is not wasting its time by saying "being interpreted is, God with us." The Bible is specifically making a point.

- Colossians 2:9: "For in him dwelleth all the fullness of the Godhead bodily" (KJV). The pronoun *Him* refers to Jesus; the word *Godhead* refers to the Almighty Spirit of Jesus, which is the Spirit of Almighty God. How can I say this? Well, we must learn by scripture and get it understood: there is only one God, one Spirit, and one Salvation. This would be God our Savior.

As the Bible states in 1 Timothy 2:3: "For this is good and acceptable in the sight of God our Saviour" (KJV). But we are taught by the Word of God that Jesus is our Savior, and Jesus is the Word of God. This is rightfully so. He is also known as the Holy Spirit. This is rightfully so. What we sometimes forget is that Jesus said, "I and my Father are one" (John 10:30 KJV). They are one—one in Spirit. Remember Colossians 2:9: "in him [Jesus] dwelleth all the fullness of the Godhead bodily" (KJV). Remember Matthew 1:23: "God with us" (KJV). Remember, 1 Timothy 3:16: "God manifest in the flesh" (KJV). What flesh? Jesus's, of course! The body is a vessel. His true identity is the Holy Spirit that dwells in that vessel, not only for Jesus, but for everyone on this planet who is in Christ Jesus. The body is a container;

the Holy Spirit is in that container. The expression of the Holy Spirit is who we truly are, *if* we are in Christ Jesus.

By our actions, we reflect our Spirit. Don't get me wrong; we are now still of the flesh, with a fleshly spirit. If we have accepted Christ, we are adopted into the family of God, our Father in Heaven. His Spirit is dwelling in us. This can only mean one thing. We are in constant battle with the fleshly spirit, through the Spirit of Christ. This is all confirmed by the book of Ephesians chapter 6. Read it in your Bible. In the foreknowledge of God, our Father, He sees us complete in Christ. We are all one in Christ, as Christ is one in the Father—one spirit in the family of God our Father. This knowledge is first mentioned in the book of Genesis, chapter 3 verse 22. Read it in your Bible.

In the life of Jesus, the created Son of God, Jesus, the anointed vessel of God our Father, would reflect the perfect image of the Almighty invisible Holy Spirit in every Word He spoke, and every action He made.

Jesus was a witness to the Word of God our Father. Jesus was and still is the living Word of God. How can I say this? John 10:30: "I and my Father are one" (KJV). Jesus is speaking of His Spirit always, not His physical being His fleshly body. He is the Holy Spirit!

So many things sound like contradictions in the Holy Word of God. But in this earthly and physical world, as the body and Spirit are together as one, so are the Father and Son. The Father is the Almighty invisible Spirit; the Son was created by that Almighty invisible Spirit and is the earthly anointed vessel that brought us the intimate knowledge of that invisible Spirit. Only through the life of Jesus, the created Son or anointed vessel, which contained the fullness of God, with no measure, can we identify and have an intimate relationship with God our creator as our Father in Heaven.

We have bodies, souls, and spirits here on this planet. The soul is a record of life being expressed by the body and spirit. God is our Father, the Almighty invisible Spirit, the Son, a created anointed vessel for that Spirit, to witness to us and express by that life the fullness in Spirit of God our Father. A recorded book of that Spirit, as the Word of God, is the Bible, wherein we can know Him (God) as our Father, not just the Almighty God, creator of all. The Holy Spirit we receive is a gift of God's Holy Spirit; we receive it through Jesus the Christ, if we believe.

Jesus was also created for the purpose of sacrifice for our sins. God our Father, who is Holy, will not tolerate sin at any time. He cannot. God our Father is a pure and clean Spirit. When Jesus cried out on the cross, "My God, my God, why have thou forsaken me?"(KJV). I believe at that time, the fullness of the Father's Spirit had to leave Jesus (God's anointed earthly vessel) as Jesus took on the sins of the world. Jesus was created for this purpose. I believe that, at this time, Jesus the fleshly vessel, may have felt forsaken, because He said, "I thirst." I do not believe Jesus was actually thirsty for water, though He may have been. I believe He had a thirst for the Father's Spirit, that fullness and comfort of the Almighty Spirit. I also believe that the sponge that the Bible tells us had been soaked in vinegar and gall also contained a drug. This, of course, would have been unclean, and a full example of sin. I believe that, the moment Jesus took a sip of the liquid from that sponge, He took upon Himself the sins of this world.

One might say, if God cannot tolerate sin, how could He have entered into a body of flesh? The body of flesh would carry the sins of Adam and Eve through the bloodlines. This is true. In all other men, this would be true; it is not possible to be born without sin. But with Christ, it is different. How? Mary, His mother, came from the bloodlines of natural sin. This bloodline came from Adam and Eve. This caused the mother of Jesus to have a sinful nature also. But Mary was a virgin, and her child was conceived by the Holy Spirit, the Spirit of our Father in Heaven. The anointed vessel inside of Mary received the created blood of God our Father. Note that, inside a woman experiencing a healthy pregnancy, the fetus does not receive, or carry any of the female's blood at any time. Not at all. This means that, from conception to birth, it is only from the male's part in conception, the created blood is developed in that vessel, the fetus, or body. Medical science does prove this. Research it for yourself! If the woman's blood does enter, it may be life threatening. The medical term is, Rhesus isoimmunization.

So a created vessel—in other words, a body from a virgin— would be a clean and pure vessel for the Spirit of God our Father, because God will not tolerate sin at any time. Also, this proves the shed blood on the cross was God's created blood for our salvation.

So even now, after all this said, you might ask, how can Jesus be God, if He is to sit at the right hand of God? This is to be explained in a spiritual understanding of the dispensation of the church Age of Grace. First of all, know that God our Father knows all things from start to finish, even before they ever exist. We can spiritually understand the truth through His Holy Word, the Bible.

After reading the Bible, from Genesis to Revelation, we can truly understand and believe God knows all things, even before they ever became reality or even exist. How can I say this? Well, in the beginning of the Bible, we learn what God already knew, before it ever existed, but by the end of the books of the Bible, we know how all things will end. Realize now that we know how it ends, even though it hasn't happened yet. We know and believe it through the spiritual Words of God. It is a done deal, finished, and complete—in the knowledge of God, of course. But as Christians, we can understand the completion of His work, and of His Holy scriptures. This would be to understand why it reads in Genesis that God Almighty Himself created the world in six days, but yet also reads, in Genesis 1:26 "let us make man in our image" (KJV). Or in the book of John 1:10 "He [Jesus] was in the world, and the world was made by him, and the world knew him not" (KJV). These scriptures may sound like contradictions, but they are not, we must understand scripture! Jesus is the Almighty Holy Spirit!

The Bible was not written in one specific year or in one single location. The Bible is a collection of writings, and the earliest ones were written nearly 3,500 years ago. The first five books were written by Moses. Moses lived between

1500 and 1300 BC, though he wrote of the events of the first eleven chapters of the Bible that occurred long before his time, such as creation and the great flood of Noah. The earliest writings began when symbols were scratched or pressed on clay tablets. The Egyptians refined this technique and developed an early form of writing known as hieroglyphics. The Bible tells us Moses was educated in all the teachings of the Egyptians. So he would have been familiar with the major writing systems of his time. Moses also received the two tablets of the Ten Commandments (Exodus 31:18). This information brings us to the conclusion that the earliest writings in the Bible were written around 1400 BC. Through the centuries, the foreknowledge of God's Word was written by many different authors from many different walks of life, but yet they lived centuries and decades apart. They all came to one understanding and truth in the completion of the Holy Word of God, the Bible. It is all to be understood in the specific dispensation, or time of a reality, even if it had not been a reality, or even existed. Knowing this truth, I can understand why we say, God the Father, God the Son, and God the Holy Spirit. Or we read, "let us make man in our image." Or, "Jesus, the created son of God, created the world was in the world and the world knew Him not." Or, "Jesus sits at the right hand of God." This is all true, by the teachings of the scripture. This is all true in its dispensation of time. Knowing this truth, I pray we all can understand why the Bible states that Jesus sits at the right hand of God. Like everything in the Bible, we have to put our understanding to the specific dispensation of the scriptures—content. I will explain.

At the beginning, Adam and Eve had only one commandment from God: Do not eat from the tree of knowledge. This would be a dispensation for a time period.

At the time of Noah, the world was flooded because of sin; this was, you might say, a purification. This also was a dispensation, or a time period.

At the time of Abraham, God called Abraham and his family out from among his people, because Abraham was a just man in the sight of God. God made a promise of a covenant to Abraham, and the Jewish religion was eventually established. Before this happened, no one was known as a Jew. This, of course, was to establish the beginning, or the root, of an intimate knowledge of the one and true God. This was a dispensation, or a time period.

At the time of Moses, when God called him to lead his people, now known as Jews, out of Egypt, God gave Moses the two tablets of the Ten Commandments, which are known as the law. Now his people could read the law and know if their actions were sinful, even if they did not feel in their consciences that their actions were sinful. His people were now under the law. This was a dispensation, or a time period.

Then came Jesus from the Jewish bloodline of Abraham to King David. Jesus was also born a Jew and brought up in the Jewish religion. He and His family were all under the law. Note: Jesus of the flesh was called the son of David. He was raised as a Jew in the fleshly worship known as the Jewish religion. This is why He is called the son of David, by the Old Testament's knowledge of worshiping God, but

Jesus was of the New Testament. He is of the Spirit of the Father. He came to abolish a fleshly religion and replace it with a spiritual knowledge and relationship with the Father.

Animal sacrifices, of course, were still an offering for the atonement of sin in the Old Testament. Jesus, of course, knew no sin, because He was the perfect anointed vessel, or Son of God, who would take the blame for our sin, and pay the ultimate price, which is death. He died in the flesh in our place, so we could live forever in His Spirit—if we believe! This was a dispensation, or a time period.

After the death, burial, and resurrection of Christ came the mystery of the Church Age, or the Age of Grace for all humankind, Jew or Gentile. Jesus paid the price; He fulfilled the scriptures and the law as man could not. Jesus, God's Holy Spirit in the anointed fleshly vessel, conquered the flesh. God defeated sin for man and took it upon His fleshly vessel. He took our place for the guilt of sin. He, who knew no sin, became sin in our place of judgment. We must know and believe we could never fulfill the law. If we break the least of the commandments, we break them all. Why? Sin is sin, no matter how large or small. God is perfect and sinless. So then also is the place in which He dwells, Heaven. So then how could any human born with a sinful nature enter into Heaven? By the blood sacrifice of Jesus Christ, our Lord, God, and Savior. If we truly understand and know this truth, we are saved by the grace of God only. Nothing else! If we think we are good enough to please God by our works in life, by our conduct, or how we try to please and help other people, then our efforts could be in vain. Jesus, the fleshly vessel, who was the likeness of sin, but had no sin, said, "There is none good but my Father in Heaven." It is not what we can do, but what Jesus Christ did for us. I believe and understand that this is to please God. To not understand this as truth is to call God a liar, and to say that Jesus died in vain. Are we that sure of our righteousness and goodness that we think we can top the life of Jesus, God in the flesh, the created anointed vessel of God Almighty, the Son of God? I don't think so. This is why we need Jesus. Because He offers us His grace and eternal life. This is a dispensation, or a time period.

The Bible states many times that, after the death, burial, and resurrection of Jesus Christ, the Son of God, Jesus sits at the right hand of God. Well now, if we are going to believe that Jesus is God, how then does He sit at the right hand of God? Could Jesus be another god, as the New World Translation states in John 1:1? I don't think so. Another god? No way, no shape, no form. There is only one God, and no one else—remember the scripture. So what then, you might ask? Well, what did we learn from the scriptures? God our Father is the Almighty Spirit, and He created a pure and clean fleshly vessel to enter. Why? To teach us, so that we would know Him as our Father. The vessel had to give up His life and shed the created blood of God for our sins. Why? Because God our Father is the creator of all. It was His plan, and the only way man could come to know Him intimately. Therefore, it was His responsibility, and His alone. Now, when Jesus went up to Heaven, as in the beginning, He went in a glorified body, not a body of flesh. We will do the same one day. So as of now, we spiritually see Jesus sitting at the right hand of God. This is a dispensation, or time period. Jesus was always in glorified form before He was ever born of the flesh.

After the Church Age, or Age of Grace. The saints of God, or the believers in Jesus Christ, will all one day be in Heaven, or the kingdom on Earth. When we go to Heaven, even if it were tonight, are we to see Jesus sitting at the right hand of God? I don't think so. What do the scriptures teach us? Jesus was God in an anointed fleshly vessel. 1 Corinthians 15:28 and John 15:23 of the (KJV) help us understand. In Corinthians it says, "And when all things shall be subdued unto him, then shall the son also himself be subject unto him that put all things under him, that God may be all in all" (KJV). (The sentence of the scripture says that God may be all in all.) In John 15:23 we learn, "He that hateth me, hateth my Father also" (KJV). This tells me that God and Jesus will be as one. We as saints will not only recognize Jesus as the Son of God, or our Savior Jesus, but as God our Father. As He taught us by His life and death on Earth, they will be one in Spirit in fullness, as it was before the foundation of the world. This is why we can read, "God Almighty created the world." Then we read, "let us make man in our image." Or in the book of John, "Jesus created the world was in the world and the world knew Him not." All of the scripture is in reference to one Spirit, God's Almighty Spirit, brought in human form so that we could intimately know Him as our Father. This is why Jesus says in Revelation 1:8 "I am Alpha and Omega" (KJV). This is why the name of Jesus is the greatest in Heaven or on Earth. This is why He will be the King of Kings and Lord of Lords. This is why Jesus said, "I and my Father are one"

John 10:30 (KJV). Because they are just that: one God, one Spirit, and one Salvation. They are, as 1 Corinthians 15:28 states, "all in all" (KJV). As one Almighty Spirit God our Father. Remember, all things were known to God before the foundation of the world. Remember all things are complete in the foreknowledge of God. Jesus said it on the cross: "It is finished" John 19:30 (KJV). So was the role of Jesus as the Son of God, as the servant. Now we will see Him as God Almighty, as King of Kings, and Lord of Lords. How can I say this? Isaiah 9:6 states, "For unto us a child is born, unto us a son is given: and the government shall be upon his shoulders: And his name shall be called Wonderful, Counsellor, The Mighty God, The Everlasting Father, The Prince of peace" (KJV). Isaiah 9:6 tells me what 1 Corinthians 15:28 confirms—that Jesus, the Father, and of course the Holy Spirit, are all in all! They are one Spirit who is God Jehovah, God Almighty, our Father in Heaven.

Our Father created the world. When we are born into His world, He gives us life; it is free. We surely don't do anything to deserve to be born in His world, but He does give us life. This life we have now is limited. But, by His Holy Word, the promise of eternal life is also free. We cannot do anything in the flesh to deserve this free gift, and nothing to earn it. It is free eternal life. The first life is of the natural. The second is of the Spirit. It is supernatural!

If we come to know Jesus and believe the Words of the Holy Spirit, which are our Father's Words, by believing the life, the death, the burial, and the resurrection of Jesus Christ, we then freely receive the second birth of eternal spiritual life. Look at these scriptures. John 6:45 reads, "It is written in the prophets, And they shall be all taught by God. Every man therefore that hath heard, and hath learned of the Father, cometh unto me [Jesus]" (KJV).

John 6:40 reads, "And this is the will of him [the Father] that sent me, [Jesus] that everyone which seeth the Son, and believeth on him, may have everlasting life: and I will raise him up at the last day" (KJV).

John 7:16 reads, "Je'sus answered them, and said, My doctrine is not mine, but his who sent me" (KJV). When Jesus spoke these words, the people hearing these words were of the flesh. They could see only the flesh, the person Jesus. What they didn't know, and some of us still don't realize, is that Jesus is of the Spirit. He is speaking the Words of the Spirit, which are of the Father. So when Jesus says, "… or whether I speak of my own authority," what He is referring to is that the eyes of the flesh only see flesh, but Jesus was of the one and only Almighty Spirit, God our Father. John 10:30 reads, "I and my Father are one" (KJV). I believe the scriptures have taught us in the everlasting dispossession, or in the completion of all things, that we who are now with the Father, in perfect union with His Holy Spirit, will forevermore see Jesus, who was once known in the flesh, as the Son of God, as our Father. How can I say this? Remember that every word of scripture Jesus spoke was the Father's Word. Jesus was always identifying the Father. This is why we will see Him as the Father. Jesus said it Himself: "when you see me, you see The Father, I and my Father are one." One God, one Spirit, one Salvation—Jesus the Christ!

Praise be to God our Father.

Identifying the Spirit of God

In this study, I will be speaking and sharing scripture of one Spirit in three identifying functions that form the members, which are many. This would be, of course, the body of Christ, the church. God Almighty is the creator of all. We, as the church in Christ, are the many functions within that Almighty Spirit in this world and the world to come. We are the expression of God's invisible Spirit, as Jesus was, as God on Earth in the flesh. We are not perfect and sinless in the flesh as Jesus was, because we are not God in the flesh. But, if we believe in Jesus Christ as our Lord and Savior, we are, in His sight, the Spirit of Christ. Therefore, we are seen by our Father God as the sinless flesh of Jesus the Christ.

The first thing in scripture we must see and understand as a reality or fact is that God our Father is, alone, the creator of all (Isaiah 45:18). We must also understand that our Father God is the Word (John 1:1: "and the Word was God" KJV). We must also know and understand clearly what Isaiah 9:6 is telling us plainly. By all scripture we can understand these titles! Matthew 3:17 reads, "This is My beloved son, in whom I am well pleased" (NKJV). In each scripture you must keep in mind what is understood in all scriptures. Each scripture is like a gear that fits so perfectly into the gears of all other scriptures. Now with all scripture, or gears, turning to one complete revolution, each gear should fit perfectly and come to one spiritual understanding. Note that I said a "spiritual understanding"! Don't use your carnal mind. Think of all scripture as a whole, or as I said, all gears turning perfectly to one complete revolution, which leads us to one complete revelation and understanding of the Word of God. To have this revelation is to have a spiritual knowledge of the Word of God. This is given to us from God our Father. In your text, or Bible, each scripture must relate perfectly. If it doesn't, then something is wrong. In some translations of scripture, the words are changed drastically from the original text.

The Lord said, "Seek me diligently." If you read only one translation of the Bible, or follow one faith or denomination of what is called religion, then you may never find truth. If your faith, or religion, is so strong in your heart and mind, you may feel solely convinced you need not to look anywhere else. If you are correct in your judgment, by all scripture of your translation, praise be to God. But, if your translation is not clear to satisfy your understanding of all scripture, something is wrong. If your translation has been altered by adding to or subtracting from the original words, or adding a complete new understanding of the New Testament, I would strongly suggest you seek Him diligently.

Now back to Matthew 3:17: "This is My Son, of whom I am well pleased" (NKJV). First, as I said, all scripture must lead us to one truth of understanding. John 3:16 states, "For God so loved the world that He gave His only begotten son, that whoever believes in Him should not perish but have everlasting life" (NKJV). Think of all scripture. This is truth. Jesus, the anointed vessel of flesh, or the Son of God, was indeed created by our Father, the Holy Spirit. Think now, how was He created? Why, of course, by the Word of God. We know Jesus as the Word of God, because He brought us the Father's Word in human form! God our

Father was very pleased with His creation of Jesus, as He was with the world He had created. He was so pleased and loved the world so much, He came as man, but perfect and sinless. Why did He do this? Because of human free will. The choice of life often led to sin, and sin led to death. You might ask, so why would God give us a free will to begin with? Because He is a loving God, not a dictator of force. You might say, if I have to believe in Jesus as my Savior, or else I'm damned to eternal damnation, isn't that by force, leaving me with no choice? Well I have to say this, if you don't know the Bible, or what it teaches, then I can understand your thoughts. But, if you knew the Word of God, you would plainly see and understand the love and the mercy of our loving Father, our Savior (1 Timothy 2:3)!

God knows our every thought. He knows our lust for life. He knows of our sin. God gave us a way of salvation, not by force, but by choice. Look at it this way: We of the flesh, even with the Holy Spirit dwelling in us, are still capable of committing sin. The difference is, we will grieve in our Spirit of Christ and feel the shame of sin, whereas before we knew the Word of God, and the Spirit that came to dwell, we might think nothing of that sin. Maybe even boast of what we have done in sin.

The Bible says the Lord our God will put His Ten Commandments in our hearts, not on tablets of stone, (2 Cor 3:3 NKJV). This means you will grieve and know you have done wrong. Why? Because the Spirit of God is dwelling in you. This is when you know He has paid in full for your sin. You cannot read a commandment from God and obey it, or feel the sin if you commit it. But if the Word of God is in your heart, His commandments will feel just and righteous and worthy of being obeyed. This is free will, or choice.

God knows we are still of a sinful nature, because of the fleshly spirit and its overwhelming desires. The stronger we grow in the Spirit of God, the less we will fail and give in to the desires of the flesh. This is why the sinless and perfect body of Christ Jesus was nailed to a cross. He took our place on that cross. We are the ones who have free will, in weakness of His Spirit, with the lust of sin to fulfill all fleshly desires. But He gave us a free gift of the Holy Spirit, the Word of God. All we have to do is believe it. If we receive the gift of the Holy Spirit, He will dwell in us. We will change our way of thinking; the Holy Spirit will strengthen us. This is how we realize we are of a sinful nature. Then we can ask Jesus to take control of our lives. He will not steer us wrong. He will change us in due time. As we grow in His Spirit with the knowledge of His Word, we will become more Christ-like in His Spirit. This would be a true love from humankind, given back to God our Father. So why was God, so well pleased with His son? Because He was pleased to serve His creation, with the cup of His own blood, from the perfect and sinless body of Jesus the Christ, His anointed earthly vessel! Read Colossians 2:9 and John 3:34 in your Bible. Also 1 Timothy 3:16 of the King James Version, which reads, "God manifest in the flesh" (KJV). He was well pleased with His son, because He could now fulfill scripture. 1 Timothy 2:3 of the King James Version reads, "God our Saviour."

Praise be to God.

I Am a Christian

First of all, there is one very important scripture a Christian must know, understand, and believe. This scripture is Luke 22:42: "Saying, Father, if it is Your will, take this cup away from Me; Nevertheless not My will, but Yours be done" (NKJV).

One might ask, why should this scripture be at the top of my list as a Christian? Pay close attention to the scriptures. The scriptures will explain.

- Matthew 1:23: "and they shall call his name Emmanuel, which being interpreted is, God with us" (KJV).
- 1 Timothy 3:16: "God was manifest in the flesh," (KJV).
- John 1:14: "And the Word was made flesh, and dwelt among us," (KJV).
- John 3:16: "For God so loved the world, that he gave his only begotten son," (KJV).

Now you might ask, what these scriptures have to do with Luke 22:42. First of all, every one of these scriptures pertains to the flesh. Remember, Jesus was flesh! His Spirit was of the Father. Now I have been through all of this in *My Study*, but what we are to focus on as the scriptures speak is the flesh—and the *natural* spirit of the *flesh* as well!

Luke 22:40: "And when he was at the place, he said unto them, pray that ye enter not into temptation" (KJV). Think about this deeply! Jesus was human—as of the flesh. Jesus experienced in His life all of the sorrow, hardship, pain, suffering, and temptation any of us would, especially on the night of His betrayal. He was sweating drops of blood, perhaps because of the great emotional torment He experienced as a man. Remember, Jesus was experiencing this as a man, a fleshly man with a natural spirit. The difference in the anointed vessel of Jesus was the fullness of God's Spirit, as well, with no measure. This truth we find in Colossians 2:9 and John 3:34 (KJV). The anointed fleshly vessel, Jesus, was created by the Almighty Spirit of God. He was born into the world by the fleshly vessel, Mary, His mother. This is why the fleshly vessel, Jesus, is known as the Son of God, the Almighty Spirit of God. Also remember, the Almighty Spirit God Himself entered the fleshly vessel, Jesus, which made Him Jesus, the anointed one, God in the flesh! Why? To conquer the spirit of the flesh, of the natural, which is sinful! Also remember, Jesus was in the likeness of sinful flesh, but knew no sin. Also remember, Jesus as a man of flesh, took on Himself the sins of the world. Only God Almighty Himself could do this. We wrestle with two spirits in this life as a Christian. We are of the natural spirit, but as Christians, we have received the Holy Spirit, and we wrestle the natural spirit to keep it under subjugation. The Bible teaches that we are one in Christ, as Christ is one in the Father. This, I believe, is, in truth, the foreknowledge of God. All things are complete with God and were known to God before they ever existed in this world. In the everlasting dispensation of time, as we Christians would be in spiritual form, we will be complete, one in Christ, as Christ is one in the Father. As for now, in this world, as flesh, we are not. This is why we wrestle continuously with two spirits as Christians. In the foreknowledge of God, only through the blood of Christ, if we believe, God our Father sees us perfect, as the Spirit and anointed vessel of Christ Himself. Therefore we are complete in Christ, in the foreknowledge of God. This is why we read that we are one in Christ, as Christ is one in the Father. I also believe this is why we are called the body of Christ. We, as Christians, are the expression of the Holy Spirit in the world today.

So I believe when Jesus said to His disciples, "Pray not to fall into temptation," it was because Jesus Himself felt the weakness of the flesh and the temptation. Remember, His disciples had fallen asleep. They surely were not worried about falling into temptation. I believe Jesus said this because the spirit of temptation had fallen on Him. (Of what? Backing out!) How can I say this? Luke 22:42: "Father, if thou be willing, remove this cup from me" (KJV). What cup? His blood for the New Testament! I would like you to spiritually think about this: In this world—the natural, the physical— we are taught by scripture to store up our treasures in Heaven (1 Timothy 6:17–19 KJV). In this world, men for centuries have searched for the Holy Grail. If it were to be found, it would be considered a priceless artifact. With a spiritual mind, think deeply on these words. The cup from which Jesus drank is indeed priceless. Why? Because we cannot buy salvation; it is freely given to us. As Christians, we have found the Holy Grail. It is the true treasure we store in Heaven. It is the gift of salvation, the grace of God.

Now you may be thinking, what is this all about? Where are you going with this? It is not so much where I'm going, but where I'm coming from, to where we are now.

Let me explain *religion*.

Jesus the Christ, as the grace of God our Father, has taken us out of the flesh-offering religion to a spiritual union with the Father. In the Jewish religion of the Old Testament, animal sacrifices were offered as an atonement for sin. Why an innocent animal would be put to death, his body eaten by the priest, his blood sprinkled in this religion of the flesh? The way I see it, this practice was all symbolic to the death of the cross. Think about this: Abraham was willing and ready to give the life of Isaac, his promised son. What do you think was going through Abraham's mind and heart? He must have thought, *why? I have always served you. I have received the promised son, who is to be the father of many nations. How can this be?* But, Abraham knew that God could have taken Isaac anyway. Then, not understanding and fearing God, Abraham was determined to act upon the command of God. Brokenhearted of course! I believe it was the love and the fear of God that compelled him to act, but what happened? God stopped Abraham and supplied a ram for the sacrifice. So now, if a man of flesh with a sinful nature was willing to give up his son for God, how much more would God do for man? This, of course, would be just an example of the ultimate sacrifice. Well, the way I see it, God had to do it all Himself! God had to become flesh in order to conquer flesh (or sin), and had to give of His own flesh as the price of redemption.

The Old Testament religion was one of flesh sacrifice, so, in my understanding, I refer it to a flesh religion. Jesus came to change this kind of worship from a flesh-giving perspective to a spiritual knowledge of the Father. Think about this: Every man from the bloodline of Adam is a sinner. The flesh is sinful. To be a Christian, we must spiritually kill the flesh—or the sinful spirit—so that the Spirit of our Father will reign.

Do you see any resemblance of the Old Testament? If not, you soon will! The flesh is sinful; this is why the Spirit of our Father will put it under subjugation to His Spirit, in the anointed flesh vessel of Christ Jesus. As in 1 Corinthians 15:28, the Spirit of our Father will put the flesh in its place (the natural). Even though the flesh was first and the Holy Spirit second, in our human form the Holy Spirit will reign first in our temple of flesh. Then, by His grace, as the foreknowledge of God, we will be complete in Christ. We will be one in Christ, as Christ is one in the Father, so that God may be all in all!

On Abraham's altar, the sacrifice was a ram, but on the cross it was the anointed earthly vessel, in the likeness of sin, Jesus of God our Father, the Almighty Holy Spirit. He is our ransom!

Luke 22:19: "And he took bread, and gave thanks, and broke it, and gave unto them, saying, This is my body which is given for you: this do in remembrance of me" (KJV). Do you see the resemblance to the Old Testament? Yes, I can, but we will not physically eat His flesh. The bread signifying the Word of God, eaten by humankind, will, in fact, be the body of Christ or the Word of God. This is all spiritual understanding.

Luke 22:20: "Likewise also the cup after supper," (KJV). This refers to verse 17, the fruit of the vine, saying, "This cup is the New Testament in my blood, which is shed for you" (KJV). Do you hear these words: "My blood shed for you"? Remember, Jesus was the invisible Spirit of God in the anointed fleshly vessel. It was His created flesh, or vessel, and His created blood. Another thing we just don't realize is how much God wanted to sacrifice His earthly vessel for us as the ultimate ransom, so that then, and only then, He could be our Savior, our mediator, our Father. Jesus expressed these feelings in Luke 22:15: "And he said unto them, With desire I have desired to eat this Passover meal with you before I suffer:" (KJV). Do you hear these words, *with desire*? Jesus knew He was to suffer, to be humiliated, to be beaten unmercifully, to be spit upon, but worst of all, to be the ultimate of our sin, then nailed to the cross. An innocent man, who knew no sin, paid the penalty for sin. With the shedding of His blood, He paid in full for the sins of this world. This means all who are of the flesh must recognize Jesus's shedding of blood for redemption of their sins.

Now I want you to think very deeply on these words: Jesus was flesh when He said, in Luke 22:42, "Father, if thou be willing, *remove* this cup from me:" (KJV). But, our God is an awesome God, with Almighty power. His Spirit, which is Almighty, is in Christ, expressing the Word in action. Saying to the flesh in the last part of Luke 22:42: "nevertheless not my will, but thine, be done" (KJV). This is an example of what I see taking place here in the scripture. As Christians, we received the Spirit of Christ in us. If we truly received His Spirit, and feed it daily with His Word, we will be strong to resist temptation. An example might be, if a Christian were down on his luck and needed money badly for his family, he might fall into temptation. Let's say this Christian walked into an unoccupied room. On the table was a very expensive Rolex watch. Now he may think, *I could sell this, and have the money I need. No one would ever suspect me.* But, as the thought might occur, it would be destroyed by the Almighty power of the Lord's Word dwelling in him. For the commandments of God are in his heart, not just written for one to see. He would say, "Not my will [as of the flesh], but your will be done [as the Spirit of Christ dwelling in him]." This is the power and integrity of the Holy Spirit within him that would keep the flesh under subjugation.

So why is Luke 22:42 so powerful and a must to understand? Well, here it is: If Jesus had not been God in the flesh, He could never have gone to the cross willingly. If He was not God in the flesh, He could not have conquered the flesh. Knowing the Spirit of God our Father is Almighty, He did, completely, put the flesh spirit under subjugation to His Holy Spirit. As Christians, we must realize that the cup Jesus drank from in the physical form as flesh, so that, when we, in a spiritual action, eat the bread and drink of the fruit of the vine, we will remember His cup was to die and shed His blood for us as a New Testament. As said in Luke 22:20: "this cup is the New Testament in my blood, which is shed for you" (KJV). Do you hear these words? If you do, then you know the teachings of Paul in our Father's New Testament. We are saved by grace and nothing else. How can I say this? Luke 22:20: "This cup is the new covenant in My blood, which is shed for you" (NKJV). Paul is our New Testament disciple. God changed him, as He will change us. Paul hated Christians; he had them put to death. God, the Holy Spirit, conquers all flesh that is sinful and unknowing of God our Father.

So as the Holy Spirit taught Paul, Christ Himself, so did Paul teach Peter, who had been a disciple of Christ. Peter knew Jesus as a man, as the Messiah. Paul did not even meet Jesus in the flesh, and neither do we. He knew Him only through the Spirit, and so do we. Do you know the story of Paul on the road to Damascus in the book of Acts? If you don't, go to the book of acts and read about Saul, whose name is changed to Paul. Paul preaches the one, true, and only gospel for the Church Age, or the Age of Grace. Matthew, Mark, Luke, and John are the four gospels most commonly taught. We learn and profit by these gospels, but these gospels were directed to people of the Jewish religion. This, of course, would be people of the Old Testament. Even though Matthew, Mark, Luke, and John are written scripture in the New Testament that we read, they pertain to life as it was in the Old Testament. The New Testament is after the death, burial, and resurrection of Jesus Christ. Paul received the Gospel of Grace from the Spirit of Christ Himself, as we do today, from the word of God. Read the story; it is amazing.

Jesus told Peter, in Luke 22:32: "and when thou are converted, strengthen thy brother?" (KJV). This, of course, is when Peter understood the teachings of Paul, our New

Testament disciple. We are saved by grace and nothing else, if we believe Jesus is:

- Our ransom
- Our redeemer
- Our mediator
- Our salvation

The Word of God was made flesh to witness the Word, so by hearing the Word, by faith in Christ, we are saved. But again, why is Luke 22:42 so important? Think now, deeply! If Jesus was only a man, or if Jesus was the Son of God as a separate entity, or as the New World Translation states, another god, where is the Almighty power, the all-knowing, the Almighty Word of God our Father? The Almighty power to defeat the flesh! Jesus was the living Word, as anointed flesh, as a man. He of flesh did express the weakness of the flesh. As said in Luke 22:42: "take this cup away from Me;"! But, as the power of the Holy Spirit, He said, "nevertheless not My will, but Yours be done" (NKJV).

Why? It was the righteousness of God our Father. He created the world. He gave humankind a free will. He was responsible for the salvation of humankind. Not Abraham, or his son Isaac, and not another entity or god. Sure, Abraham would have sacrificed Isaac, but why? For the fear of God. Sure Abraham loved and served God, but if the fear of the Almighty God was in mind, and the ultimate reason to carry on, I don't think this would have made the mark. For it was out of love, and love alone, that God gave of His son, His own and only earthly vessel, the only begotten Son born of anointed flesh. Remember, if God our Father is not

Almighty enough to give of Himself, to experience the pain and suffering of humankind, which He created, *surely* no other god is!

This is why we must know: one God, one Spirit, and one Salvation. If Luke 22:42 had not happened as it reads, I don't think I could understand, as a man of flesh, how the love of God our Father could have saved me from my sins.

What is the understanding of truth and the Word of God? *Salvation*! This is to be adopted into the family of God, our Father in Heaven.

Praise be to God.

Flesh and Spirit

What I will try to explain is the likeness of humankind to the likeness of God our Father, who dwells in Heaven, who is the creator of all. In this world, humankind and all the animals are flesh. God did create humankind, and every living mammal, reptile, fish, and bird with flesh, bone, and blood. He breathed into them life, and they became living souls (Genesis 2:7). From the knowledge of all scripture, I believe God gave all creatures life in the same manner. The great difference is God created humankind in His perfect image. Adam and Eve in the beginning knew no sin. They came to know sin after eating from the tree of knowledge. Because of this knowledge, they now would experience sin. Now because of sin, they no longer would be in the perfect image of God. Adam and Eve now would be of the natural world. Like any other living creature. For Adam and Eve, or humankind to regain this perfect image. One must eat from the tree of life. Genesis 3:22 "And the Lord God said, Behold, the man is become as one of us, to know good and evil: and now, lest he put forth his hand, and take also of the tree of life, and eat, and live for ever:" (KJV). I believe God's love has forgiveness for all, if they will come to His calling. I also believe the soul is the record or evidence of any creature's life. But, for humankind it is of great and important value to have a perfect record. This of course, is why we need Christ Jesus. His blood will cover our sins. The Almighty Holy Spirit will see us as sinless as His earthly anointed vessel Jesus Christ. We are now reborn in the perfect image of God. This is why we are known as the body of Christ.

I am not claiming to know all the mysteries of life, but I am claiming what I understand from the Holy Scriptures, the Bible, which is the Word of God!

Let's start with Adam and Eve. They were flesh, as every living creature in this world. The great difference is the spirit. The Bible doesn't teach us that animals have spirits, although we often refer to a horse of high spirit, or one of a calm and gentle spirit. We often liken the character of an animal to what we sometimes refer to as its spirit. It is my understanding that we do this because, as humans, the spirit in motion is the actions of the flesh. For it is what comes out of a man (in Christ), or a natural man's heart that defiles him (Matthew 15:18–20 NKJV). I cannot say that, by the Word of God, animals have spirits, but I can say that God did give them life, and they are of the natural world. I can say that every animal has its own identity and character. Animals may have spirits, because they do have life, but it would not be in the likeness of God.

Three dogs will have their own individual characters, as will three cats, or three horses. I'm sure you get my point. Now, whether animals have a spirit or not, one thing is for sure—it would *not* be in the likeness of God our creator. You may decide for yourself. I will try to explain flesh and spirit in the likeness of God our Father. You may see some resemblance of flesh in action in the animal world that relates to us humans.

The Bible teaches that God created man in His image (Genesis 1:27). But it also reads in verse 26, "let us make man in our image" (NKJV). We might look at this and wonder. The Bible also teaches God is Spirit, and He is invisible. We are all of flesh; we are visible. We might ask, what image? I will explain how, by the foreknowledge of God, He made man in His image. First of all, it must be understood that Adam and Eve were created as mature adults, although they were, in fact, as little children in the Garden of Eden. They were very much like children of today. They knew nothing of sin. They were innocent in mind and heart, and had not a worry in the world. God, like our parents today, took total care of them. Like babies, or young children today, Adam and Eve were innocent to life. Now, as adults, the parents are not innocent. Parents know—or should know—right from wrong. As an adult, you are accountable to God and humankind for your actions.

This is how I see it. Adam and Eve, innocent of sin, or life as we know it today, had one commandment from God: Do not eat from the tree of knowledge! But Satan came and tempted them, and they did eat. Today, the more you tell a child not to do something, the more the child will want to do what you ask it not to do.

Satan said to Eve, Genesis 3:5 "For God knows that in the day you eat of it your eyes will be opened, and you will be like God, knowing good and evil" (NKJV). Note that he did not say she would know good *from* evil. This is important to remember, because there is a difference. The scripture does go on to say, "You will be like God, knowing good and evil" Genesis 3:5 (NKJV). Well, if that doesn't beat all. Doesn't this sound like an adolescent, a teenager, today? They just can't wait to grow up. They already think they know it all, but that's not good enough. They want to be just like their parents—to be considered as adults, not realizing that the parents are still taking full care of their needs, and no way can they do for themselves. Even so, they want their own authority, and to live as of their own will. Keep in mind they are children, wanting to be adults. I see the same picture with Adam and Eve. They thought they could be like God.

So why were they so foolish? Adam and Eve were like innocent children, but wanted to know all that their creator did—good and evil! Through this, they became adults, accountable for their own lives, as well as their souls. When they learned good and evil, they had to choose between good and evil. Here's where the big problem starts. They were of the flesh! The will to satisfy the flesh is overwhelming. If you are hungry, you will eat. If it is something that is very tasteful, you may eat too much, then say to yourself, why did I eat so much? If you are thirsty, you will drink to satisfy that need. You will satisfy the flesh in all aspects of life.

Now, Adam and Eve had to choose good from evil, but that is not so easy when the will of the flesh is so demanding and must be satisfied. Remember, they were on their own to choose right from wrong, good from evil. Being able to know good and evil, they did in fact teach good to their children, but they also had to teach what was evil. This is the same today! We are taught right from wrong as children. So if we have the knowledge of good and evil, and still choose evil, it is because we have no power of the Spirit of

Jesus Christ dwelling in us. This, of course, would be the foreknowledge of God in the future of humankind to come centuries after Adam and Eve.

This is why sin grew rapidly in the world after the fall of Adam and Eve. At the time of Noah, centuries later, evil, or sin, was great in the world, but good also did exist in the knowledge of men such as Noah. God saw him as a righteous man. God was going to destroy the world and every man and woman. But, because of one man of flesh, to be called by God a righteous man, God gave all a way of salvation. Sadly, no one could hear the words of Noah. His words were not satisfying to their flesh. The righteous words of Noah were foolish to the hardened and sinful hearts of the unsatisfied flesh of a sinful world. I say unsatisfied, because without the true knowledge of good, the flesh will reign in full authority to fulfill its never-ending lust for life.

So now that we have, in part, the fulfillment of the scriptures, I hope everyone can understand why God our Father had to come to us as flesh. It was His creation and His plan. The free will God gave humankind often led to sin, and sin led to death. God our Father wanted humankind to love Him by choice, not by force. He had to come in the flesh as humankind. He came for three reasons.

The first reason was to live the life as human and experience all in life that humankind did. He would be tempted by sin, or by the flesh. He would suffer the hardships of life as anyone would. This would be a just and righteous God. Remember, it was His plan and His creation. So then it had to be His responsibility, and His alone. He came in the flesh

(1 Timothy 3:16) to live as fleshly man, but to live a perfect, and righteous life. Humankind could not, so God did it for them. God our Father came to conquer the flesh, or sin. This is why Jesus said in John 10:30: "I and my Father are One" (KJV).

The second reason God our Father came as flesh was to sacrifice His fleshly body. This would be for the redemption of sin, which comes from the sinful flesh of humankind.

The third reason was to show us by His existence here on Earth, as Jesus, His anointed vessel, or created son, the Spirit of the one, only, and true God—the Spirit of God our Father who dwells in Christ, His anointed created vessel, or Son. Colossians 2:9: "For in Him dwells all the fullness of the Godhead bodily;" (NKJV) [the flesh vessel Jesus]. John 3:34: "For he [the anointed fleshly vessel, Jesus] whom God has sent speaks the Words of God, for God does not give the Spirit by measure" (NKJV). This tells me that Jesus was 100 percent the Spirit of God our Father in a flesh vessel, as 1 Timothy 3:16 states. Why? So we could all know God personally as our Father, just as Adam and Eve did before they were on their own. God our Father is Spirit; John 4:24 tells us this. The life of Jesus shows us this truth. By looking at the life of Jesus, we can see our Father in reality of His teachings and His actions. By the death of Christ, if we believe, we are made as righteous as Adam and Eve were before they knew good and evil. We will receive the Spirit of Christ, His Holy Spirit. This will give us the power to control the lust and spirit of the natural flesh. For the law of God our Father will be in our hearts. His Spirit will reign over the spirit of the flesh. The power of God's Spirit will choose good from evil. The Spirit of God our Father was given to us from the knowledge of Jesus the Christ. His Spirit dwells in us as the Spirit of God our Father dwelled in Christ. Then, and only then, are we the adopted sons, or the children of God our Father. Our spirits then are of the Holy Spirit. It is not 100 percent as Christ of the Father, but it is 100 percent in the sight of God our Father, for he has made us righteous through Christ in His sight. Why? Because we believe in Christ, the anointed fleshly vessel of God Himself. John 14:17: "the Spirit of truth, whom the world cannot receive, because it neither sees Him nor knows Him; but you know Him, for He dwells with you and will be in you" (NKJV). Do you hear and understand the words of this scripture? It is so critical to understand this very important scripture!

Remember, Jesus showed us who the Father is. By His life here on planet Earth, we know the Father, who is our Savior. 1 Timothy 2:3–4: "For this is good and acceptable in the sight of God our Saviour; Who will have all men to be saved, and to come unto the knowledge of the truth" (KJV). Without that image of the Spirit of God our Father, brought to us from the life and knowledge of Jesus the Christ, we would be like all the animals of this world. We would be the natural created human. We would be, flesh, bone, and blood, with a natural earthly spirit. God our Father has made us in His image, through the image of His Spirit in Christ—if we believe! The foreknowledge of God is first mentioned in Genesis 3:22, as it reads, "And the Lord God said, Behold, the man is become as one of us, to know good and evil: and now, lest he put forth his hand, and take also of the tree of life, and eat, and live forever:" (KJV).

Some animals have a pecking order. This would be to show others who is the most dominant, the one who would take control, the one who would overpower the others. I see this every day in the behavior of my horses. If I feed them in a field in buckets spread out some twenty-five to thirty feet apart, I will see the same horse finish his feed then run to the next bucket and take whatever feed, if any, is left in the bucket. Then that same horse will run to the third bucket as well, chasing off the other two horses. This, of course, is to satisfy his own need. What need is that? The lust of his flesh!

Many animals will react in the same manner, but I have seen two horses eat from the same trough, as well as two dogs eat from the same bowl, and cats as well. So what am I saying? No, I am not saying that some animals have righteous spirits. Perhaps the animals that submit to the most dominant do so in fear of a bloody conflict, or even death. The most dominant, perhaps, doesn't think of the consequences. This animal would only want to fulfill its desire, which is the lust of its flesh! To fulfill that need, the flesh is demanding.

So you might say, what is this animal thing all about? Take a good look at humankind as a whole, without the image of God our Father's Spirit dwelling in us. We are just like any other animal on this planet. How can I say this? Use your mind. Think of what I'm saying. Humankind, for decades now, has done its best to close the book of knowledge, of wisdom, of truth, and righteousness—yes, the Holy Bible, the Word of God our Father. The penalty for this is sin. This world has not seen such great sin and taken it so lightly since the time of Noah and the great flood. You might say, but sin has always been in the world. If so, you are close, but not on target. Sin came when humankind had to *choose* good from evil. Remember Adam and Eve? How they wanted to be like Daddy, our Father in Heaven?

We of the Church Age, or the Age of Grace, have the Spirit of God our Father within reach. We have only to ask for it, and search for it. Then His Spirit will dwell in us. Only through the life of Jesus Christ, if we believe, are we made righteous in the sight of God our Father. The Church Age, or Age of Grace, is a very unique dispensation of time. There has been none like it before the death, burial, and resurrection of Christ. There will be none like it after the rapture, or second coming of Jesus Christ. You might say, I don't believe in a rapture. Or you might say that the second coming has passed. If so, this can only be a religious doctrine. The rapture and the second coming of Christ are ahead. It is my opinion, as opinions go, that you should seek Him diligently. All scripture pertaining to the rapture, and Christ's second coming has not been fulfilled as yet. I pray you will get out of your box of religious doctrine and seek Him diligently. You cannot seek Him any further in the space of your religious box. Your box contains only the beliefs of your doctrine. You will constantly face the four walls of your doctrine. Whether it be truth or error, what you see is what you get, and nothing more. Climb out and seek knowledge everywhere! Seek Him diligently!

We are still flesh and capable of sin, but we press on to live in the Spirit of God our Savior through the knowledge of Christ (Philippians 3:14 NKJV). This will keep the flesh under subjugation. We will not be sinless or perfect, but our hope is to be so. Without the Spirit of God our Father, we are like two dogs in the street—a male and a female, ready, able, and willing to fulfill the lust of the flesh, then go their separate ways. The female may end up with puppies to care for, but the male is out to care for his next lustful need. Do you see the resemblance to our society today? As for the female dog, if she were a woman, she just might have her babies killed. This, of course, would be abortion. Her need may be to go on fulfilling her fleshly desire—not the desire to raise her children, but to satisfy her desire of lust with another night out in the street! Come to Christ; God will forgive you.

In these last days, this has become acceptable to those who do not have the Spirit of God our Father. Good has become evil, and evil has become good in the sight of man. How can I say this? *Roe versus Wade* has made it legal, since 1973, for over 55 million babies to have been killed in their mother's wombs. This is barbaric and evil! But humankind's law says it is good and just for the woman's choice. This is why we need the Spirit of God our Father to dwell in us—so that we may have the wisdom and knowledge to choose good from evil. We cannot conquer the flesh, as Jesus did, but with His Spirit, we will keep it under subjugation. Without the Spirit of God our Father, through Jesus the Christ, we are nothing more than flesh as any other animal. We will react in life in the same manner.

Our society today has accepted sin and thinks nothing of its consequences, just as in the time of Noah! One might say that all this talk of the lust of the flesh is only about a natural instinct of human beings. I must say, I can agree with you, more than you may know. The Bible teaches us that first there is the natural, then the spiritual. We are born of the natural, but we must be reborn of the Spirit. Need I say anything more? The truth of this statement is first mentioned in Genesis 3:22: "And the Lord God said, Behold, the man is become as one of us, to know good and evil: and now, lest he put forth his hand, and take also of the tree of life, and eat, and live forever" (KJV). This plainly tells me that we are first born of the natural. This, of course is flesh, bone, and blood, with an earthly spirit! We must be reborn in the Spirit of God our Father. This does not make us perfect and sinless. In this life we fight against the spirit of the natural with the Spirit of God our Father that dwells in us through Christ. The truth of this statement is in Ephesians 6:11–12: "Put on the whole armor of God, that ye may be able to stand against the wiles of the devil. For we wrestle not against flesh and blood, but against principalities, against powers, against the rulers of the darkness of this world, against spiritual wickedness in high places" (KJV).

I believe the spirit world is very real. How can I say this? The Bible teaches us that God is the Almighty invisible Spirit. He is the Holy Spirit, which is righteousness in truth of the Word of God. The Word of God, of course, would be the foundation of His identity. It is all power and authority. We are taught by scripture that Jesus is the Word of God.

This is rightfully so! Why? Because Jesus was the anointed earthly vessel of the Almighty invisible Spirit. How can I say this? John 1:10: "He was in the world, and the world was made by him, and the world knew him not" (KJV). John 1:14: "And the Word was made flesh, and dwelt among us" (KJV). 1 Timothy 3:16: "God was manifest in the flesh" (KJV). Matthew 1:23: "God with us" (KJV).

John 1:1: "In the beginning was the Word, and the Word was with God, and the Word was God" (KJV). Note that the word *with* is not to be understood as "alongside of," but rather as "together as one, all in all"! If the Word is all power and authority, which it is, then it is the Almighty Spirit of God. No Word, no God! The anointed earthly vessel Jesus brought us the Spirit of God our Father in truth. Jesus was flesh and Spirit in His creation. Why? We are flesh and spirit in His creation. Jesus brought us the knowledge of the Word of God. This is why He is called the Word of God. He expressed in His life the Word of God. John 4:24: "God is Spirit, and they that worship him must worship him in Spirit and in Truth" (KJV). Jesus brought us this knowledge. He is the perfect image of Almighty God in Spirit. If we are in Christ Jesus, by the foreknowledge of God, in the completion of all things, we are in that perfect image of God.

No matter how great or small the sins of our flesh may be, Jesus brought us the knowledge of our salvation. The earthly vessel, pure and sinless, which contains the fullness of God our Father in Spirit, was crucified in place of our sinful flesh. This is why Jesus said in John 3:17: "For God sent not his son into the world to condemn the world; but that the world through him might be saved" (KJV). Also Acts 2:21 reads, "And it shall come to pass, that whosoever shall call on the name of the Lord shall be saved" (KJV). This, of course, is the anointed sinless vessel of God Himself, known in the world as the Son of God, the Son of Man, the son of the David, the Word of God, our Savior, Jesus. To understand this fully is to understand that Jesus, the anointed vessel of flesh, was the all-knowing, the all loving, the all merciful, the one and only Almighty God Jehovah, our Father in Heaven!

If you do not see my thoughts and opinions on the subject, then please watch documentaries on the Discovery Channel and Animal Planet. Then you may see my point. As you watch, just keep in mind what humankind would be without the Spirit of God dwelling in us.

Praise be to God.

God Have Mercy

Yes, I have come to thee, from the blessed fruit of My sacred choice,

I have planted My seed in the Earth, of My divine will,

I have sprouted a tender shoot, among tall grass in the fields of life,

I have grown in glory, with tassels of seed,

I have sown in truth, for My creations need,

I have nourished the Earth, with the riches of soil,

I have seen her grass, and her rays of splendor,

For My mercy all I have given, for those who surrender!

We often use the expressions "God, have mercy" or "Lord, have mercy." It is great that we acknowledge our creator, God our Father. We may fail to realize He has already given us all the mercy within Him. He gave it all at the cross, in the likeness of sinful man. It is now up to us to accept the love and mercy of God our Father. What some of us may not realize is that God our creator gave 100 percent of Himself for us. How? By coming as man, His creation, but to live a perfect life for humankind. Jesus in the flesh is the anointed vessel of God who brought us the knowledge and mercy of God—if we believe!

Think about this, and I do mean think: If God is Almighty (and He is!), it had to be Him and Him alone on the cross. The Bible teaches us that Jesus was the created Son of God, the Almighty Spirit. This is true! We also must consider all scripture and what it teaches. If you look at Matthew 1:23 very closely, you will see it is making a specific point: God with us (KJV)! This of course would explain 1 Timothy 3:16: "God was manifest in the flesh" (KJV)! Also, John 1:10: "He was in the world, and the world was made by Him, and the world knew Him not" (KJV)!

When we read scripture, we must remember that God our Father is Almighty. To say He is Almighty is to realize that, when we speak of the Word of God, we are speaking of His Almighty Word. This, to my understanding, would be His Almighty Spirit in action. John 4:24 says, "God is Spirit." So when we read John 1:1: "In the beginning was the Word and the Word was with God, and the Word was God" (KJV) it is so easy for me to understand John 1:14: "And the Word was made flesh, and dwelt among us, and we behold his glory, the glory as of the only begotten of the Father, full of grace and Truth" (KJV). Think about this! When John 1:14 states, "and the Word was made flesh," it is saying that God the Father, who is the Almighty Word, was made flesh. Then it says, "and dwelt among us" (KJV). This, of course, would be His created son, Jesus, who was His anointed fleshly vessel. Then it says, "and we beheld his glory" (KJV). Now, whose glory? Why, of course, the Father's glory, because

He is the Almighty Word. But then it says, "the glory (-- as of--) the only begotten of the Father, full of grace and truth (KJV). Do you see how this is stated? "As of--- the only begotten." To me this is saying that Jesus of the flesh, was the "only" anointed earthly vessel born in the world that would contain the fullness in Spirit of God our Father. Jesus brought us the Father's glory in the world-- as of—the Son of God. How? He was the Holy Spirit in the body of the only begotten Son made of flesh. He was begotten from Mary, His earthly mother. (Matthew 1:23 "God with us" NKJV). Jesus was God the Father, as the only begotten son. Note once again how this anointed vessel is showing us who the Father is, through the life of Jesus Christ, the created Son, because John 1:14 says, "as of the Father, full of Grace and Truth" (KJV). By this scripture alone I can fully understand John 1:1 and John 1:14. The knowledge of all scripture will explain one specific scripture as a whole, but if you let your religious background steer you in your understanding, then you may fail to see the black-and-white truth of what the scriptures are teaching us.

We have to understand, if God our Father is Almighty, then, of course, all is of Him, and Him alone. He crucified His fleshly body, His created son Jesus, because it was His will. Why? So that through the life of Jesus, we could know our God and Father. Then, by knowing Him and trusting in Him through the life of Christ, we are made righteous in His sight. Then and only then can we have the Spirit of Christ dwell in us. Then and only then are we in His sight as children of God our Father. We are now reborn! We were once born in the natural birth from our mother's womb, only with a natural spirit, but now we are born of His Spirit. We will no longer see life as we once did. We are reborn of His likeness in Spirit, not completely in the fleshly spirit of this world. He crucified His flesh physically so we could spiritually crucify our fleshly spirit daily! This is only by the power of the Holy Spirit that dwells in us. This is the power to keep the fleshly spirit under subjugation. We are not sinless, but by His Spirit in us, we will not live a life of lust in this world, which is sin.

Read and understand the scriptures of Titus 3:4–7: (KJV).

> "But after that the kindness and love of God our Saviour toward man appeared [this, of course would be Jesus, His created son] Not by works of righteousness which we have done, [meaning we cannot do anything to justly earn salvation] but according to his mercy he saved us, by the washing of regeneration, and renewing of the Holy Spirit [which I believe means to be cleansed of our sinful life, and reborn in the Holy Ghost;"

The next two scriptures confirm my understanding: Titus 3:6–7: "Which he shed on us abundantly through Je'sus Christ our Saviour; That being justified by his grace, we should be made heirs according to the hope of eternal life" (KJV).

It was God Almighty's fleshly body on that cross full of grace and truth. All we have to do is believe His love and mercy. The Bible says in John 3:16: "For God so loved the world that He gave His only begotten son" (NKJV). This is true, but what do the scriptures teach?

Matthew 1:23: "Behold, a virgin, shall be with child, and shall bring forth a son, and they shall call his name Em-man'u-el, which being interpreted is, God with us" (KJV)!

1 Timothy 3:16: "God was manifest in the flesh" (KJV)!

John 1:14: "And the Word was made flesh and dwelt among us" (KJV)!

John 1:10: "He was in the world, and the world was made through Him, and the world did not knew Him" (NKJV)!

John 10:30: "I and my Father are one" (KJV)!

John 14:7: "if you had known me, you should have known my Father also, and from henceforth [or from now on], you know him, and have seen him" (KJV)!

Colossians 2:9: "Four in Him [Jesus] dwelleth all the fullness of the Godhead bodily" (KJV)!

John 3:34: "four He whom God had sent [Jesus] speaketh the Word of God, for God giveth not the Spirit by measure unto him" (KJV)! (100 percent God)

1 Timothy 4:10: "For therefore, we both labor and suffer reproach, because we trust in the living God, who is the Saviour of all men, specially of those that believe" (KJV)!

1 Timothy 2:3: "Four this is good and acceptable in the sight of God our Saviour" (KJV)!

John 1:1: "In the beginning was the Word, and the Word was with God, and the Word was God" (KJV)!

2 Corinthians 5:18–19: "And all things are of God, who hath reconciled us to himself by Je'sus Christ, and hath given to us the mystery of reconciliation. To wit, that God was in Christ, reconciling the world unto himself, not imputing their trespasses unto them; and hath committed unto us the Word of reconciliation" (KJV)! Note: Do you see how it is written in verse 18—"all things are of God"? Do you notice that, in verse 19, "God was in Christ, to reconcile the world unto Himself"? These two verses alone confirm all the scripture above! But, if it's not clear yet, I have two more verses.

Deuteronomy 32:39: "Now see that I, even I, am He, And there is no God besides Me;" (NKJV)!

Isaiah 9:6: "For unto us a Child is born, Unto us a Son is given; And the government will be upon His shoulder. And His name shall be called Wonderful, Counselor, Mighty God, Everlasting Father, Pince of Peace" (NKJV)!

Now, after reading and studying these scriptures alone, I can surely see the love and mercy of Jehovah God, our Father. He came in the flesh as a human, in the likeness of sin, but having no sin. He came so that humankind could relate to Him in full understanding of who He is. Remember, Jehovah God is an invisible Spirit. But as human, the anointed vessel of God, He could teach us scripture in the person of the Son of God. A human of flesh was now able to see and hear the actions of His Almighty Spirit. Through the life of Jesus, humankind could be shown the intimate knowledge of the will, the love, and the mercy of Jehovah God our Father. He, God our Father, so loved the world He came as the only begotten son—Jesus, our Savior! The Almighty Holy Spirit!

Praise be to God.

The Love of the Father

This will be plain talk, common sense, and knowledge in the Word of God our Father. When we read His Word brought to us by His son, or His anointed vessel, Jesus the Christ, we are taught by the Word of God. When Jesus spoke, He spoke in the Spirit of the Almighty God our Father. Jesus was created for this purpose.

Why did God our Father want us to know Him intimately, as family? We all truly know and love our immediate families. Why? Because we know them intimately. If we lose someone we love, we are heartbroken. If we learn of the death of a friend's friend or family member, but we have no intimate relationship, we still feel the loss and sorrow for that person and his or her family. We may not feel the heartbreaking sorrow of that loss. The reason is intimacy. We either have it or we don't.

God our Father has this intimate love for everyone in this world, and I do mean everyone. He created us. He knew us long before the foundation of the world existed. We could not have this intimate relationship with our Father in Heaven without the life of Jesus the Christ. Jesus brought us the love of our Father. Jesus shows us by every action and every Word He spoke who our Father is.

Jesus said, "I and my Father are one." Jesus said, "I am in Him, and He is in Me." Jesus said, "when you see Me, you see the Father," the (NKJV and the KJV) state this very much the same. Now, I have been through all of this. But again why would Jesus say these things? Because He is the Father! He is the Son! He is the Holy Spirit! How else could we say we love God, if not by the life of Jesus the Christ?

I am not one to say I believe in a trinity, or as it may be called, a three-person God. I believe in only one God, my Father in Heaven. This is what the Bible teaches. I can say He is the Father, He is the Son, and He is the Holy Spirit. How is this so? By the one and only, the Alpha and Omega, the always and everlasting Almighty Spirit, my Father in Heaven. He demonstrated His intimate concern and love for us, by the life, death, burial, and resurrection of Jesus Christ, His earthly created anointed vessel, or Son of God.

The Bible teaches us that God our Father came into His created world as a human—the man Jesus. Jesus was flesh, a man of the Jewish faith. This is why He is also called the son of David, or the Son of Man. He is also, of course, known as the Son of God. Why? Because He is the Christ, the Savior of His creation, the Holy, Almighty Spirit of God the Father. Can you see the love of our Father through the life, death, burial, and resurrection of Jesus the Christ? He wanted us to know Him with an intimate love, like He has for us. How else could we truly know Him, if He had not come as human, a man?

The love of our Father is so great, so overwhelming, it is hard for us to truly comprehend its magnitude and depth. He loved us while we were yet in sin, the Bible teaches. Think about this! If people do us wrong continuously, it is hard for us to like them, much less love them. The love our Father has for us is beyond explanation.

Think about your life and how you have lived, or even now how you may be living outside the Word of God. We are not perfect; we are all sinners. This is because we are of the fleshly spirit. The flesh is overwhelming with its earthly desires. We are tormented with the temptations of the flesh. Some we win, and some, sad to say, we lose. But it is not our Spirit in Christ to lose to temptation. The stronger we are in His Spirit by the Word of God, the less we will fail. Paul said that our life in the Spirit of Christ is like running a race. If we fall down, we must get up and finish the race. It doesn't matter if we come in first or last, we just must finish.

Jesus told the woman caught in adultery, John 8:11 "Neither do I condemn you; go and sin no more" (NKJV). Does this mean this woman would never sin again for the rest of her life? Of course not! Jesus is telling her, "Go, but follow me, don't follow your fleshly lusts of life. Follow the Spirit of life everlasting." This is the awesome love of our Father. When we give Him our lives, we are saved. If we fall, He is there to pick us up. If we do not give our lives to Christ, we will continuously fall. He will not be there to pick us up and place us back in the race. He may pick us up, because of His awesome love. But, if we were not in the race of faith in Christ, we will remain on the side as a spectator. Join the race Paul speaks of. We are not perfect, but Christ was in His earthly life. He lived a perfect and sinless life because we cannot. This is the awesome love of God our Father. He who believes in Christ shall have eternal life.

Now think deeply on these words, of how much God our Father loves us. If you can see and feel the awesome love of that great sacrifice known to us as Jesus Christ the Son of God, then truly bury your thoughts in these words: It was God Himself on that cross, in the likeness of sinful man. Why? The number one reason is His awesome love for us. Think deeply of what the scriptures teach through the black-and-white letters that describe the Son of God, Jesus the Christ.

God our Father, the Almighty Spirit, created everything known and unknown to humankind. He is the creator of all. It was His Almighty, Holy Spirit that spoke His Word for all creation. Jesus was that Word brought to us in human form. This is why He is known as the Word of God. The Bible teaches that Jesus was with God in the beginning. Well then, back up in your thoughts. The Word of God, Jesus, or the Bible and its contents were all known to the Almighty Spirit before it ever existed in life for humankind. I believe Jesus, in His glorified form, was in Heaven, as one with the Father before He was ever born on Earth in the flesh. How can I say this? If God our Father is an invisible Spirit, He had to have the image of His created man in order to speak face-to-face with man, as He did with Abraham and Sarah when He visited with them and told them of the promised son, Isaac. Read Genesis 18:1-14 in your Bible. It was our Lord, and two angels. Do you remember the scriptures? Perhaps Abraham did not look directly into the face of the Almighty; I don't know. I know only that the Bible states it was our Lord.

Moses asked our Lord if he could see Him face to face (Exodus 33:17–23) read it in your Bible. The Almighty God of Heaven said no, but He promised to show Moses His backside. Then, as Moses was backed into a cave, the

Almighty passed by the opening of the cave, and Moses saw His backside. This would have been the glorified and spiritual vessel of God our Father—the Christ, our Savior! The creator of all! God our Father! How can I say this? Because the intimate knowledge and love of the Father had not yet been brought to humankind. This is why Moses could not see Him face to face; it was not the time. Why? Because the scripture had not yet been fulfilled.

The intimate knowledge of our Lord was not known to humankind, because it came when Jesus was born of the Blessed Virgin, here on planet Earth. Then and only then was the intimate love and relationship brought to humankind, face to face. This, of course, would be the Church Age, or Age of Grace. Before the birth of Christ, humankind did not know God intimately as our Father, only as an Almighty Creator of all, Holy and just, and worthy of all. Read Galatians 4:1–9. This scripture plainly tells me that the people of the Old Testament—both Jews and Gentiles—did not know God intimately before the birth of Christ. Jesus said it Himself. John 8:19 "If you had known Me, you would have known my Father also" (NKJV). Can you see how all things changed after the birth of Christ our Savior, God in the flesh? Humankind worships not only the one and only God Almighty, but now, through the life, death, burial, and resurrection of Christ, we know Him in an intimate relationship of love, as God our Father has always had for us. This is what makes a family. This is what forms the closeness of an intimate love. This is how we can be heirs with Christ. We, through Jesus the Christ, are adopted into the family of God, our Father in Heaven.

Only through the blood of Christ, if we believe, may we enter into our spiritual home. The Earth is not our home. It is only a place for us to learn of the love of our Father. If we love the lust of this world more than what our Father has done for us, or what He has claimed for us, then we may never receive our inheritance—the inheritance of all His creation, known and unknown to humankind, along with an eternal life. Note: People say we come into this world with nothing, and leave with nothing. This is not completely so! We do come with nothing, but in Christ, we leave with everything.

Why an eternal life? Think about this: Life is the knowledge of existence. Death is not. Here is a very small example of what I'm saying: If you walk into a dark room, you cannot see; therefore, you cannot explain the existence of what is. But if you turn the light on, then all is exposed. You now can see, and by seeing you can now feel and explain the existence of what is now known to you by the light. This is life eternal: to always and forever know the existence of creation, and the love of our Father, the creator of all. Jesus said He was the light of the world. Why? Because in the darkness of lust in this world, we cannot see life eternal. But, with the light of Jesus, the Word of God, we can see the love of our Father and all He has promised. This is the awesome love of God our Father. So with that said, you may feel, in the reality of your innermost being, which is your spirit, the awesome love of our Father in Heaven. If Jesus was only the Son of God, a separate entity, or even another god as the New World Translation teaches, where, then, is the love of God Almighty, our Father in Heaven? Go now to Isaiah 9:6.

Read it carefully. I pray our Lord will give you His light so that you will see through the darkness of the doctrines of many manmade religions. Follow your religion if you will, but please turn the light on! For the love of God, don't get lost in the darkness.

Praise be to God.

Religion

First of all, let's see what the Webster's New World Dictionary has to say. Religion is "a set of beliefs concerning the cause, nature, and purpose of the universe, especially belief in or the worship of God, or gods." Religion is "an organized system of belief in and worship of God or gods." Religion is "something one believes in, or follows devotedly."

Well, now it is not religion that saves us. This is plain and simple understanding to me. Think about this—the world is full of religion. In my opinion, the Bible is the Word of God and the knowledge of God. But there are many religions and gods to choose from. Think about this as well—let's say religion is like a box. You are in a box when you follow religion and its doctrines. If you do not get out of the box and seek Him diligently, all you will know is what is in your box. The four walls of your box are the doctrines of your religion. You will bounce off the walls of doctrine. In your box, you will not find any knowledge other than what is stored in your box. If you want to seek God diligently, you will have to climb out of your box, or at lest stick your head out.

Now, I am not advising that you forget your religion. I am simply advising you to seek knowledge of the Word of God. How can you do this? Do not close your ears to other understandings of God's Word. My knowledge is merely the understanding of my thoughts, which is an opinion. We all have the right in America, as well as within the will of God, to an opinion. This, of course, is free will, given to us from God. If you are strong and sound in your beliefs of God's Word, then nothing I say, or anyone else says, can move you. But I pray that your understanding is from the Word of God, and not doctrines. The Bible teaches us in 2 Corinthians 13:5 that we must examine ourselves to see if we are in the faith. Only scripture can give us truth about ourselves. All scripture together should explain one isolated scripture. If all scripture does not mesh perfectly to all scripture, then something is wrong! It may be the translation of your Bible, or the denominational teachings of scripture. To truly know and understand all scripture, we must search all Bible text. We must hear the words from all religions of the world. Then read the Bible text. But keep in mind there is only one God, one faith, one baptism if God is Almighty, and He is! There can be only one God. The world has many religions and many gods, but there is only one truth, and one God.

People born in a country where the majority of people believe in a particular religion or god usually adopt those same beliefs. Why? Family tradition. A culture of people will always follow their ancestors. The history and ancestry of a culture of people is reason enough to blindly follow a religion. One might think, *If our religion was good enough for our grandparents, and Mom and Dad, then it's good enough for me.* Why is it so easy for one to feel this way? In most cases it is the intimate love and devotion of a family, and the trust and comfort expressed in life that all is well.

In this great country of America, we have the freedom to choose our religion. This is why we are a great nation. It does not matter where our family ancestry originates. We are Americans; it is our freedom to practice our religious beliefs.

We are a country of many cultures and religious beliefs. This is what makes America a free nation. If the United States government ever chokes the voice of any religious group, it will choke to death the freedom of America.

Some may disagree, but America was founded as a Christian nation. How can I say this? Study a little history. You will learn that the Holy Bible was most likely taught in the early settlement schools of America. In some of our old movies, scriptures from the Bible are often expressed. Many of our forefathers often quoted scripture in their beliefs concerning this great Nation of America. I also can plainly see that our great American Constitution was written in parallel to the laws of God. It is my belief that America was, and still is, a Christian nation. Now when I say Christian nation, for the most, I refer to a religious belief. Why? Because there are many flavors of Christian belief. If one suits your taste, you will follow it, especially if your family has for decades. Religion is something one practices to find favor with God. Your favor offered to God by your religious acts may not please God at all. In fact, it may even anger Him. Why? Because we cannot do anything to please God except to believe what He has done for us. Remember, He is the Almighty one, not us. We cannot buy eternal life by good merit. In all religions of the world, people do good merits, many truly believing the merits are the will of God. But, in fact, the merits or actions they physically express because of this religious belief may be evil and totally against the will of God. The most likely reason this could be is that there is a book that describes what is known as a religion.

Let me say this about religion, and how it can affect a person in this world. With the little knowledge I have of scripture, and what I understand about life in this world, I can clearly understand the life of the apostle Paul. It is my opinion that Paul, a man who killed Christians, loved God. The problem was, Paul did not truly know God. He did not have an intimate relationship with the Father. Paul knew of God only from the words of the prophets and the 613 laws of the Jewish faith, established by God for that dispensation. Paul was a Pharisee in the Jewish faith. This meant Paul was well schooled in the laws and the teachings of the forefathers of the Jewish faith. The problem was that Paul lived at a time when that old dispensation—the Old Testament—was renewed into a new dispensation, the New Testament. Paul did not understand this, and neither did Peter who had walked with Christ. Paul did not truly come to know God until he was blinded on the road to Damascus. (This clearly reflects the sentiment in the song "Amazing Grace," written by John Newton: "I once was lost, but now am found; was blind, but now I see.") Once Paul's eyes were opened to a relationship with the Father, he was schooled by revelation from Christ as to what he must preach.

Let me put it this way. Suppose there was a famous artist who painted a beautiful picture. Some saw its beauty; some could not see the beauty. The artist saw the beauty, but he also saw a terrible flaw. The artist may see that the painting, though beautiful, is not perfect enough to hang on his wall. The artist may decide to destroy it. The people of the world may disagree or agree with the artist. Think now—no matter what one thinks or believes, the artist is the only one who can rightfully destroy the painting. The artist is the one who created it; therefore, he is the only one who has the right to destroy it.

In this world there are people who follow religion blindly. Some may truly believe their actions are the will of God. Some may be following others in a religion they truly know nothing of. Some may be just plain evil with hearts to kill. No matter what the reason, these people do not have a relationship with the one and true God. Even so, our hearts should be in great concern for their souls. The Word of God teaches us to love our enemies, and to love our neighbors as we love ourselves. In understanding the scripture, this could mean only one thing. If we as Christians do not want to face damnation, then we should not want any others to face damnation.

I will try to explain my thoughts. In this world, we have many books about religion. These books of religion are based on the cultures and backgrounds of different groups of people. We have the Bible, which is in the culture and background of America. But the Bible can, or should be, taught all over the world. Why? The people of America came here from all over the world. This is what makes America the country she is. The history of the Bible is not of America or the people of America, but it is for America, as well as any other country on this planet. Why? We are all God's people by creation.

There are other books of religion, such as the Qur'an of the Muslim faith, and there are books of the Buddhist faith and the Hindu faith. These are all books of religion. They and others all teach about religions of good faith and merit. What these books lack is the history that proves the future.

This is what is known as prophecy. The Bible is the only book of so-called religion that proves its teachings. We can read the ancient history of prophecy and see it come to pass. Though it was the future, it is now history. Then now, by seeing the history that was, we can see and understand the future that is, and is to come.

This is the foreknowledge of God. This is what makes the Bible a book of knowledge, wisdom, and truth. No other book in the world can do this. Why? Because the Bible is the Word of God. The Bible is not a religion; rather, it gives us the knowledge of who we are, and who God is. The Bible will teach us where we came from and where we are going. The Bible teaches us that God is Spirit, and we must worship Him in Spirit and in truth (John 4:24 NKJV). This, to my understanding, means living a life of His Word. This is taught to us by His Word, the Holy Bible. Then and only then we will live in the spirit and truth of God our Father. This is true worship—to live a life in the knowledge of His Word, not from the teachings of a doctrine of a flavor of Christian belief, or any other religion. The Bible is not a book of religion, but a book of knowledge. All religions are manmade beliefs. This is why there are so many. If there is a religion, there should be only one, because there is only one God. But if there were no religions, everyone in the world could have a relationship as father and child with the one and only Almighty God, as taught by Jesus the Christ.

Do we live and express a spiritual relationship with God our Father, or a ritual of actions only?

Praise be to God.

Relationship

Jesus said, "I and My Father are one" John 10:30 (NKJV) and, John 14:20 "At that day you will know that I am in My Father and you in Me, and I in you" (NKJV). This is the expression of the flesh in union with the Spirit of God, our Father in Heaven. This is what an intimate relationship is—to be born of flesh, but to live in the Spirit of the Almighty God.

John 4:24 says that "God is Spirit, so we must worship Him in spirit and in truth" (NKJV). This is relationship and a true worship—to live a life of flesh, but following the guidance of His Spirit. When we are born in this world, we are born innocent of the knowledge of sin. But as we mature, we come to know sin. This is when we are accountable for sin. Some of us may realize we are living a life of sin, but because of our religious teachings, we feel God is all loving and all forgiving, so we go on in our sinful ways thinking God will forgive us. Some of us may not realize we are of sin, because the lust of the flesh has blinded the knowledge of the Spirit. The Bible teaches that, because of the lust, or will to satisfy the fleshly spirit, if we pay no attention to the Spirit of God our Father, He will turn us over to a reprobate mind. This would be to live a life blind to the knowledge and wisdom of God's Word. This would separate us from a relationship with God our Father.

To have a relationship with our Father in Heaven, as children of God, we must intimately know Him. How can we intimately know Him? By His Word, the Holy Bible. If we blindly follow a religion and never read, study, or listen to the Word of God, or have a yearning for the knowledge within the pages of the Holy Bible, how then can we say we intimately know Him, as God our Father?

God our Father is all loving and forgiving, but this knowledge is truly understood with an intimate relationship only to those who come to know Him as He calls. He is patient and all understanding of our ways and needs. He is the one who created us. He knows us well. But do we know Him? To know Him is to have a relationship with Him. This is to truly know what He has done for us even though we are of a sinful nature.

This is the love of our Father! He came as a light in the darkness of this world so that we, as blind sinners, could see and understand, by the light of Jesus, the knowledge of our Father. This is relationship—to be in union as Spirit with our Father in Heaven. Only then, by Jesus the Christ, in truth of the knowledge of God our Father, are we saved by grace and nothing else.

This world is full of religions; they cannot save you. Not even a so-called Christian religion. Religion is just what the dictionary states—one's belief of who God is. You can believe whatever you want. Your belief does not make your thoughts true facts. The Bible is a book of wisdom, knowledge, and the spirit of truth. How can we trust it as truth? Prophecy! The prophecy of the Bible will show us the truth of its contents. There are hundreds of written prophecies in the Bible. Read and study the Bible. Then and only then will you know it is the Word of God—not just another book of so-called religion, but a book of knowledge, wisdom, and truth. The truth of the Bible will join the flesh with a union of the Holy Spirit. This is a relationship with our Father in Heaven.

This would be to know Him personally; this would be to worship Him in spirit and in truth. But first we must know who we are in the flesh, before we can ever know who we are in His Spirit.

Praise be to God.

Evolution versus Creation

First of all, let me say this: I am not a scientist or one who holds a doctorate degree of any sort. In fact, I am not even the sharpest knife in the drawer; neither am I the brightest star in the sky. But I am a man who studies the Word of God. You don't have to be a rocket scientist to understand the Word of God, although, to have a mind of that caliber would certainly help in the unfolding of the mysteries of the Bible. The Bible is written in such a way that anyone can read and understand it. The problem with most people concerning their understandings of the Holy Scriptures is their education. One may try to reason an understanding rather than let the Spirit of God give an understanding. The Bible teaches that we are born of the natural, which means of the flesh. The Bible also teaches that being born of the flesh is to have a carnal mind. This would be a mind not of the Spirit of God, but of the world.

You might ask, what does this have to do with this subject? First of all, you must understand that there are two truths in this subject. One is a reality, and one is the appearance of a reality. I will do my best to explain. The Bible teaches that God created the world and everything in it. He also created the universe—everything known and unknown to humankind. The Bible teaches, by written document, that God's creation is about 6,000 years in existence. This I see as a reality of truth. Why? Because of how the scriptures read.

Science teaches that the world evolved through millions upon millions of years. Science claims that the world evolved from a big bang—a great explosion of tremendous heat and an enormous amount of released energy. This, science claims, is what placed the planets in their orbits and put the sun, the moon, and the stars in their positions as well. This all sounds good to me so far. Why? Because it sounds like the work of the Almighty God Himself—the head scientist! Anyway, to my understanding, science claims that one lump of matter bumped into another lump of matter. As they joined together over millions upon millions of years, they formed enormous bodies of matter that eventually hit each other, and this is what caused the big bang. Think about this—where did this matter come from? It would have had to come from somewhere! If this is so, where did the salt water that covers two-thirds of the Earth's surface, and all the freshwater lakes, rivers, and streams come from? Not to mention the underground freshwater streams and lakes that are on this planet. From an enormous ball of fire, we sure have a lot of water. But, as I said, I'm not a scientist. I am sure science has a theory, or an explanation for this.

What about humankind and all the animals and vegetation on this planet? Science teaches that they evolved as well, after millions upon millions of years, when the Earth had cooled and life was possible. For life to evolve, the sun, the moon, and all the planets would have had to be in just the right positions. This alone is against all odds. If you look at a picture of how the planets are situated in their orbits, you will find they all move in a circular pattern. They all follow their own precise movements, pretty much like a clock that keeps a perfect measure of time. This is why we have our four seasons. From a big bang with no control, I feel the odds are against this perfect arrangement, but let's just say this happened. But, was it without the Word of God in control?

Science teaches that man evolved from some kind of microscopic life cell. In order to have this form of life, everything that did exist had to be in the perfect environment—not close, but perfect! So just by chance from a big bang, I feel the odds are against this happening. If this is how humankind came to exist, this life cell would have to have evolved into many different forms of life. Science teaches that it took millions upon millions of years for this physical change to occur. I feel the odds are astronomical for this to be a reality.

What is even more mind-boggling is the thought of woman. What am I saying? Think about this! If it took millions upon millions upon millions of years for man to evolve, or life itself, what about woman? She is completely different from man, but yet the same being. Woman would have had to evolve at the same time as man. She also had to be compatible to man, for the reproduction of what would be known as the human being. The chances of this as a reality are phenomenal to me.

What is even more impossible to me is to think that maybe there were two great puddles of life cells. One for man and one for woman, both evolving at the same time into human form after millions upon millions of years. The world then might have had many men and women to choose from. Perhaps then we could say this is why we have all the different races of humankind. Well, I don't know if science even teaches this theory, but if science can speculate, so can I.

My point is this—if man and woman evolved separately, but at the same time, it would have had to be this way for human life to exist. But, if man or woman evolved one before the other, if only a hundred to a thousand years apart, after millions upon millions of years of evolution, the human being could not have existed. What is even a greater thought is, if man or woman evolved, they would have had to evolve as mature beings. If not, who was there to give care for the infants, to raise and care for them as we humans do today, and forever in time. The odds are not even thinkable to me! But what really disturbs me is the thought that every living thing on this planet, male and female of every creature, would have had to evolve in the same manner. Do you have any idea of the odds of this? A person could win the lottery every second of every day with these odds.

Not to mention every tree and other types of vegetation would have had to evolve at the same time as man, woman, and all the beasts, birds, and fish of this world. This, of course, would be so we all could survive. Also, remember that the trees and vegetation had to evolve in the manner of reproduction of its own kind as well. These odds, by chance, of an existing world are just overwhelming to me. I see a greater faith in strength of belief to see this as a reality! It takes more faith to believe in evolution than it does to believe in creation. All the theories of science concerning the existence of the world sound possible, but only if God Almighty our Father in Heaven, the creator of all, was in control. You might be thinking, *but science says the world has been in existence for millions upon millions of years, and the Bible teaches the world is only 6,000 years old.* This is true. I agree with the Bible as a reality. Science may see the world as what I may call the appearance of reality. I will explain my thoughts and understanding. The Bible teaches that God created the world in six days. You might ask, *Is this six literal twenty-four-hour days?* I would have to say yes. This is what the Bible teaches. Also remember, all things are taught in the knowledge of God, as the completion of His work.

I also know the Bible teaches that a thousand years is but a day with the Lord. This, to my understanding, is to show us that time is not a significant issue with God. Remember, He always was and will be. God will do whatever He wills in His own time. Remember, God is also the author of time, as well as everything known and unknown to humankind. He is the creator of all.

Now just because the Bible teaches the world was created in six days, but science claims by technology and theory the world is millions upon millions of years old, does that mean this is a reality? It is only 6,000 years in existence by the Word of God! Remember, the Bible teaches God created everything mature! This means that planet Earth was also created mature. It may surely appear to be millions upon millions of years old, even with all the great knowledge and technology of science. The world may, in fact, test out as millions upon millions of years in existence. This is no problem to me. My Father created a mature world and everything in it!

Let's just take a hypothetical look at something! We know the Bible teaches that God created Adam. Then, from Adam, He created Eve. The hypothetical thought is this: Let's say God had just created Adam. Adam was a mature man. But let's say Adam was only about six seconds into the existence of life. Now let's say, hypothetically, that God took a leading scientist of biology from this time period back to the time of Adam's creation. Now, the scientist walked up to Adam and stood only a few feet from Adam not knowing that Adam was, in fact, only six seconds into life—by creation. The first thing the scientist might do is examine the appearance of the body of Adam. The scientist would have to say, by the appearance of what he saw as a reality, that Adam was a mature man of perhaps thirty years old. Then, with a closer study of the body of Adam, by the skin texture, height, strength, teeth, and overall form of the body, the scientist would conclude Adam was about thirty years old. The scientist would then have finished his study. He may honestly state by the appearance of reality that Adam was about thirty years old. The scientist would be correct in his analysis, but wrong about the reality of Adam's age. Remember, Adam is only six seconds old in this hypothetical study. The point I'm making is this: God did, in fact, create everything, and everything was mature.

So if the world—this planet—appears to be millions upon millions of years old, I don't have a problem with that. Neither do I have a problem with any ministries of life of any sort. I don't know all the answers to all the questions. I don't have to know! If I did, then I would be like God Almighty, the all- knowing. I don't have to know. I simply have to believe! Perhaps one day in the next world, God may tell me. If He doesn't, so what? I don't have to know. I only have to believe!

It is much easier to believe in faith by creation than in the odds of evolution. Remember, we are born of the natural—the flesh—but we must be reborn of His Spirit in His likeness. This is the only way you will truly understand the reality of the teachings of God's Holy Word, the Bible. The Bible teaches the knowledge of humankind is foolishness to God. Also remember, the Bible teaches the knowledge and wisdom of God is foolishness to humankind. This, of course, would be His Word, the Holy Bible. We may believe in whatever convinces us of a reality, such as evolution or creation. But to be born of His Spirit is not a belief; it is the knowledge of God given to us who believe. This is reality!

Praise be to God.

In a Nutshell

When we study one scripture, we understand it by our understanding of all scripture. The meaning of some scriptures is as plain as the nose on your face. The meaning of other scriptures may not be so obvious. It may be that we may not understand one very important scripture in its entirety. For us to have a complete understanding of one scripture, we may need to study all scripture.

In this study, I will explain my understanding of one very important scripture: 1 Timothy 3:16. I will use only a few scriptures to explain, in truth, the entire understanding of its content. The King James Version of this scripture reads, "And without controversy great is the mystery of godliness: God was manifest in the flesh, justified in the Spirit, seen of angels, preached unto the Gentiles, believed on in [the] world, received up into glory." This scripture is plainly speaking of Jesus, but it reads, "God was manifest in the flesh."

The New World Translation of this scripture 1 Timothy 3:16 reads, "Indeed, the sacred secret of this godly devotion is adamantly great: he was made manifest in flesh, was declared righteous in spirit, appeared to Angels, was preached about among nations, was believed upon in [the] world, was received up in glory." This scripture is speaking of Jesus. The pronoun *He* is used in place of the word *God*. This is rightfully so. The scripture is speaking of Jesus. The problem is, where is the sacred secret? Throughout the whole Bible, we can read and understand that Jesus is the Word of God, brought to us in human form. In the King James Version, all scripture pertains to Jesus as the Word of God, or the Word manifest in the flesh. All scripture is complete and straight to the point. What I find in the New World Translation, with all the word changes that differ from the original translation, is that the scripture is unclear, or in fact, void. Even though these word changes have been made, I can still see the truth of what the Holy Scriptures teach. The New World Translation may be, in fact, unclear and contradictory to itself, but as a whole, I do see truth. But it is not taught as truth, in my opinion.

I will explain by the Word of God! The King James Version of John 4:24 tells us, "God is a Spirit: and they that worship him must worship him in spirit and in truth." This scripture tells me, as a Christian who has received the Spirit of Christ, we must live by that Spirit daily, and in truth of His Holy Word. This is true worship! We are still of the flesh and capable of sin, but our heart's desire should be to live in the righteousness of His Holy Word.

The Bible teaches us that God our Father is Spirit, and He is invisible. Colossians 1:15 speaks of Jesus as of the flesh, but in the image of the invisible God (NKJV). This, of course, would be of the Holy Spirit, which is the Father. I say this because of Colossians 2:9: "For in him dwelleth all the fullness of the Godhead bodily" (KJV). This would mean that Jesus is the Father in Spirit. Jesus is the created son, or anointed vessel of the Holy Spirit that is brought to us in a physical form, as a man, so that we could intimately know that invisible Spirit as the Word of God. The Bible teaches us that there is only one God, and He is Almighty. By all scripture, it is understood that Jesus is God in the flesh!

Look at these scriptures: The King James Version and the New World Translation of Deuteronomy 32:39. Both translations read very much the same. The King James Version reads, "See now that I, even I, am he, and there is no god with me." Do you see how the word *god* is written? It is written with a lower case *g*. This is the same way it is written in the New World Translation in John 1:1, as it reads, "Jesus was a god." This would mean that the New World Translation is in error, because it reads Jesus was a god, and with a lower case *g*. This is a complete contradiction in the New World Translation. When the King James Version refers to the statement in Deuteronomy 32:39, it also has a lower case *g*, but Jesus was God, with a capital *G*, as the King James Version states in John 1:1: "the Word was God."

Isaiah 45:18 of the King James Version reads, "For thus saith the Lord that created the Heavens: God himself that formed the earth and made it; he hath established it, he created it, not in vain, he formed it to be inhabited: I am the Lord; and there is none else."

Well, as I said before, that is cut and dried! Without a doubt, there is only one God! So you might ask, who is He? Is He God the Father, God the Son, God the Holy Spirit, or God Jehovah? It makes no difference! The Bible is speaking of one in the same. He is all in all, as 1 Corinthian 15:28 states (KJV). So this would explain what is said about Jesus in the King James Version in John 1:10: "He [Jesus] was in the world, and the world was made by him, and the world knew him not." This would explain how Isaiah 45:18 and John 1:10 are complete in truth. This is as plain as the nose on your face! Just read the scriptures. Colossians 2:9: "For in him dwelleth all the fullness of the Godhead bodily" (KJV). John 3:34: "For he whom God has sent speaketh the Words of God [sent or created for His purpose]: For God giveth not the Spirit by measure unto him" (KJV). Matthew 1:23: "behold, a virgin shall be with child, and shall bring forth a son, and they shall call his name Emmanuel, which being interpreted is, God with us" (KJV). Note: when the word *they* is used in this scripture, I believe it refers to the whole world. Not that we would call Him Emmanuel, but we would know Him by the interpretation, which is "God is with us"! This would truly confirm 1 Timothy 3:16: "God was manifest in the flesh" (KJV).

Think about this deeply! We are fleshly body and spirit in this world. So was the Father and created Son, together as one on earth. How else could we, as children of God, have known the Father intimately in a relationship?

Jesus tells us many times who He truly is. Jesus said in John 10:30, "I and my Father are one" (KJV). John 12:44–45: "Jesus cried and said, He that believeth on me, believeth not on me, but on him that sent me. And he that seeth me seeth him that sent me" (KJV). This scripture says *not me*, but *Him that sent me*. The Him in this scripture is the invisible Almighty Spirit, our Father God. We already know the anointed fleshly vessel, Jesus, contained His Spirit 100 percent! This is why He said, "not me" (the fleshly vessel), but "me the Almighty Spirit." John 17:22: "And the glory which thou gavest me I have given to them; that they may be one, even as we are one:" (KJV). It is all about one Spirit. Jesus is one in Spirit with Jehovah God, our Father, as we in Spirit are one in Christ Jesus. This, of course, is in the completion of all things. John 13:31: "Jesus said, Now is the Son of man glorified, and God is glorified in him" (KJV). Note that this scripture calls Jesus the Son of man, *not* the Son of God. Why? Because Jesus at this time was a fleshly vessel that glorified the Spirit of God the Father. They are one in Spirit. Jesus was 100 percent the Spirit of God the Father (John 3:34)! This scripture reads, "For he whom God hath sent speaketh the Words of God: for God giveth not the Spirit by measure unto him" (KJV). No measure! This would only mean 100 percent Spirit, the Father.

The body is nothing but a container. Your true identity is the Spirit. If you look into a mirror as a Spirit-filled child of God, you will see your enemy. Your true identity is your spirit. The fleshly vessel or body, you will see eye to eye is your enemy. Why? Because the flesh is of the natural spirit and it is of a sinful nature. This is why the perfect and innocent body or anointed vessel of God Himself was crucified in place of our sinful flesh. It was God's created blood that dripped into His created earth for the sins of humankind. This is why we say Jesus died for the sins of the world. This is why we know God our Father is Almighty. If God is Almighty, only God could ever have conquered sin for us. This is why 1 Timothy 2:3 states, "For this is good and acceptable insight of God our Saviour" (KJV). This is why John 17:3 states these words: "This is life eternal, that they might know thee the only true God, and Jesus Christ, whom thou had sent" (KJV). When the scripture reads, "and Jesus Christ whom thou hast sent," it is speaking of the anointed fleshly vessel of God. Do you truly understand these words when the word *they* is used? It refers to every living soul on this planet. The phrase "and Jesus Christ whom thou hast sent" refers to the anointed fleshly vessel, or Son of God, that is in Spirit, the one and true God. Remember, God is an invisible Spirit. He is known to us from the life, death, burial, and resurrection of Jesus Christ. Jesus was the one and true God in human form.

In most Christian teachings the terms *trinity* and *triune God* are often used. Why? I have not a clue! By these few scriptures alone, one can plainly see the Bible teaches one God, one faith or Spirit, and one salvation. But, yes, this is all known to us by the life, death, burial, and resurrection of the created son, Jesus the Christ. Who was He? I can boldly say that He was the anointed fleshly vessel of God Jehovah, our Almighty Father in Heaven. You think not? Then read Isaiah 9:6 again. In fact, read all the scripture in *My Study* again. I am not confused; I am convinced!

Praise be to God.

"Let Us Make Man in Our Image"

Well now, this is quite a statement, if there is only one God! I do mean one God, not three persons in one God, or two gods, God the Father, and a god the son, as the New World Translation teaches. The Bible teaches us that God is Almighty. To say He is Almighty is to understand there is no other. Just as Deuteronomy 32:39 states: "See now that I, even I, am he, and there is no god with me" (KJV). This is well understood. So is Isaiah 45:18: "For thus saith the Lord that created the Heavens; God [himself!] that formed the earth and made it, he hath established it; he created it not in vain, he formed it to be inhabited: I am the Lord; and there is none else" (KJV). Well, now, I believe that is straight to the point! There is only one God! So what is scripture telling us when it reads, "Let us make man in our image"?

Genesis 1:1–25 tells us how the Almighty God created all things. But, in verse 26 it reads, "let us make man in our Image" (KJV). Also, Genesis 3:22 reads, "And the Lord God said, behold, the man is become as one of us, to know good and evil: and now, lest he put forth his hand, and take also of the tree of life, and eat, and live forever." Note that this verse says, "and *now*, lest he put forth his hand, and take also of the tree of life, and eat, and live for ever: (KJV). This, of course, is a statement of the foreknowledge of God. Remember, all things were known to God before the foundation of the world. I can see that, in His mind, all things are complete. This is simply telling me that first we are born of the natural, but we must then be born of His

Spirit. This will place us in union with Him (God) as one through Christ. We are all one in Christ, as Christ is one in the Father. All one Spirit, all in all.

Well, the scriptures will certainly confuse the carnal mind. First of all, we must remember what scripture teaches us. Then we must look at the whole picture of what scripture unfolds as understanding in the realm of the Spirit. What Spirit? It is God's Almighty Spirit, which we come to know through Christ Jesus. Think now—the Bible teaches that God our Father knows all things, from start to finish, before they ever exist. All things in the mind of God Almighty are complete. Now, by faith, as Christians, when we read scripture, we also know how all things known to us by scripture will end. How can we say we truly know, and believe this? Let's just take a look at scripture, in the knowledge of God's Holy Word. 1 Corinthians 2:13: "Which things also we speak, not in the words which man's wisdom teacheth, but which the Holy Ghost teacheth; comparing spiritual things with spiritual" (KJV). I believe this means to compare scripture with scripture, then compare scripture to life itself. This would mean the wisdom of God, taught to us by the Holy Spirit, through the Word of God, the Bible. 1 Corinthians 2:7: "But we speak the wisdom of God in a mystery, even the hidden wisdom, which God ordained before the world unto our glory" (KJV). What glory? The Church Age saints, the bride of Christ. 1 Corinthians 6:15–17:

> "know ye not that your bodies are the members of Christ? shall I then take the members of Christ, and make them the members of an harlot? God forbid. What?

> Know ye not that he which is joined to a
> harlot is one body? for two, saith he, shall
> be one flesh. But he that is joined unto the
> Lord is one spirit" (KJV).

Take a look at the one Symbolic Triangle, which is Figure
D in this book. Do you understand what the scriptures are
teaching us? We are one Spirit in Christ, as Christ is one
Spirit in the Father. It is all about one Spirit. 1 Corinthians
6:19–20: "what? Know ye not that your body is the temple
of the Holy Ghost which is in you, which ye have of God,
and ye are not your own? For ye are bought with a price:
therefore glorify God in your body, and in your spirit, which
are God's" (KJV). This scripture tells me, if we are Spirit-
filled Christians, under the blood of Christ Jesus, we are
not to live as we please of this world; rather, we are to live
and please the Holy Spirit that dwells in us, for the will of
the flesh is denied for the will of God our Father. We are of
His Spirit, and not the spirit of this world. 1 Corinthians
12:12–14:

> "For as the body is one, and hath many
> members, and all the members of that
> one body, being many, are one body, so
> also is Christ. For by one Spirit are we all
> baptized into one body, whether we be Jews
> or Gentiles, whether we be bond or free;
> and have been all made to drink into one
> Spirit! For the body is not one member, but
> many" (KJV).

This scripture speaks of Christ, and He is God; we are in that Spirit, or as the scripture reads, "Baptized into one body," or as I will explain, by one symbolic triangle as that body, or family of God.

Do you understand what the scriptures are teaching us? Do you realize the fullness of its knowledge? Think now deeply of all scripture. Christ Jesus in the flesh was the glory of God in Spirit. We as Christians, in the flesh, are the glory of God in Spirit through the knowledge brought to us from the life of Jesus Christ. If we accept and believe this knowledge, we are of Christ in the glory of God in Spirit. Therefore God' the Holy Spirit, sees us as the perfect and sinless fleshly body of Christ our redeemer. We are the many members of the body of Christ Jesus.

Take a good look at these next scriptures. 1 Corinthians 2:16: "For who hath known the mind of the Lord, that he may instruct him? But we have the mind of Christ" (KJV). This would be to understand the Word of God given to us by the Holy Spirit that dwells in us. 1 Corinthians 3:16: "Know ye not that you are the temple of God, and that the Spirit of God dwelleth in you?" (KJV) This scripture, if you notice, asks you this question: Do you know it? It is all about one Spirit. 1 Corinthians 1:10: "Now I beseech you brethren, by the name of our Lord Jesus Christ, that ye all speak the same thing, and that there is no divisions among you; but that ye be perfectly joined together in the same mind and in the same judgment" (KJV). This scripture, as well as all the scriptures in 1 Corinthians chapter 1, tells me that we as Christians should not be divided. We are divided by many denominational beliefs. This, of course, is the stamped name of any religion. We should not say, I am a this, or I am a that in reference to a religion, or a denominational belief. Look at the words of Paul, in 1 Corinthians 1:12–13: "Now this I say, that every one of you saith, I am of Paul; and I am Apollos; and I of Cephas; and I of Christ. Is Christ divided? was Paul crucified for you? or were you baptized in the name of Paul" (KJV)? These two verses alone plainly tell me that we should not claim our faith by a baptism of any so-called church; rather, we should study scripture as one in Christ Jesus. Christ Jesus is our baptism! The only one and true baptism of His Holy Spirit is to accept and believe His word. For we are all one in Christ, as Christ is one Spirit in God our Father, who is the Holy Spirit. Of course, in this imperfect and sinful world, sad to say, this is not going to happen. 1 Corinthians 11:3: "But I would have you know, that the head of every man is Christ; and the head of the woman is the man; and the head of Christ is God" (KJV). This sure sounds like the Spirit of God in a chain of command, or a Godhead to me. For we are all one in the Holy Spirit. This Godhead would include the church. Ephesians 4:4–6: "There is one body, and one Spirit, even as ye are called in one hope of our calling; One Lord, one faith, one baptism, One God and Father of all, who is above all, and through all, and in you all" (KJV). The scriptures of Ephesians, and the scripture of Isaiah 9:6 come together in one complete understanding of all scripture, which is John 4:24: "God is Spirit, and those who worship Him must worship in spirit and in truth"(NKJV). 1 Timothy 3:16: "And without controversy great is the mystery of godliness: God was manifest in the flesh, justified in the Spirit, Seen by angels, Peached among the Gentiles, Believed on in the world, Received up into Glory" (NKJV). Matthew 1:23: "Behold, the virgin shall be with child, and bear a son, and they shall call His name Immanuel, which is translated, God with us" (NKJV). John 1:10: "He was in the world, and the world was made through Him, and the world did not know Him" (NKJV). This, of course, is Jesus.

Pay close attention to the rest of the scriptures in this part of *My Study*!

John 1:12: "But as many as received him, to them gave he power to become the sons of God, even to them that believe on his name" (KJV). What name? Why, of course, the name above all names in Heaven or on Earth—Jesus! Why the name Jesus? Because He is, and always was, identified with the Almighty invisible Spirit. Now what does the scripture say? It says that as many who believe on Jesus will be the sons of God. Why would the scripture say this? Because in Christ Jesus we are able to obtain an inheritance with Jesus Christ, the anointed vessel, the Spirit of God.

Listen very closely to the next scriptures; they are very important! Ephesians 1:4–7:

> (4)"According as he hath chosen us in him before the foundation of the world, that we should be Holy and without blame before him in love:" [Now, when it says, "without blame before him in love," in my opinion, this is to say, without blame in His sight]: (5) Having predestinated us unto the adoption of children by Jesus Christ to himself, according to the good

> pleasure of his will, (6) to the praise of the
> Glory of his Grace, wherein he hath made
> us accepted in the beloved. (7) In whom
> we have redemption through his blood, the
> forgiveness of sins, according to the riches
> of his Grace:" (KJV).

Ephesians 1:4 tells me that, before the foundation of the world, God Almighty knew who would come to Him in love, of His loving Spirit, known to us as the Son of God, Jesus! Then, by the sacrifice of His sinless flesh, nailed to a cross in place of our sinful flesh, we who believe would be saved by the love of His grace—God our Father in Heaven. Ephesians 1:5 tells me that, before the foundation of the world, God our Father had already adopted us as one in Christ Jesus. This would mean we are now, at this time and then, before the foundation of the world, one in Spirit with Christ Jesus. Who was Jesus? Well, by scripture, Jesus was God in the flesh. This is according to scripture. We are all one in Spirit. We are in the family of God our Father. We, as of now, are not perfect and sinless, but through Christ we are blameless. Ephesians 1:6 plainly says just that! It is by the glory of His grace that we are accepted in the family of God our Father. Ephesians 1:7 tells me plainly that we are saved only by what God our Father has done for us, which was to sacrifice His anointed flesh vessel, which was perfect, sinless, and righteous, in place of our sinful flesh.

2 Timothy 1:9–10 (NKJV).

> "who has saved us and called us with a Holy
> calling, not according to our works, but

according to His own purpose and Grace which was given to us in Christ Jesus before time began. [The King James Version says "world began."] But has now been revealed by the appearing of our Savior Jesus Christ, who has abolished death, and brought life and immortality to light through the gospel."

This is what scripture teaches us, and this is why 1 Timothy 2:3 reads, "God our Savior" (NKJV)! Jesus was God in an anointed fleshly vessel, known to us as Jesus the Christ. Note: not a three-person God in one God, or any other god, but one God in three understandings of how the Godhead works as *one*! This would also include the church! Why? Because we were adopted into His family before the world existed, and He (God) is the head of the family. We are all one in Christ, the anointed earthly vessel of God our Father. We are one in Him now, and we were before the foundation of the world. This is what the scriptures teach. This is why Genesis 1:26 reads, "let us make man in our image." This is why Genesis 3:22 reads, "and now, lest he put forth his hand, and take also of the tree of life, and eat, and live forever" (NKJV). Genesis 3:22 tells me, yes we were born of the natural, but we must be born of the Spirit of God our Savior. Remember, God knows all things from start to finish, before it ever exists. If there is only one God, and no trinity or a three-person Godhead, or any other god, then the scriptures can mean only one thing. "Let us make man in our Image" refers to God and His church, or the saints of God, in one Spirit with Christ Jesus, the Holy Spirit of God.

In Ephesians 5:30–32: "for we are members of his body, of his flesh, and of his bone for this cause shall a man leave his father and mother, and shall be joined unto his wife, and they shall be one flesh. This is a great mystery: but I speak concerning Christ and the church" (KJV). Do you understand? Do you even hear the words of that scripture?

2 Corinthians 11:2: "For I am jealous over you with godly jealousy: for I have espoused you to one husband, that I may present you as a chaste virgin to Christ" (KJV). Revelation 19:7–8:

> "let us be glad and rejoice, and give honor to him, for the marriage of the Lamb is come, and his wife hath made herself ready. And to her was granted that she should be arrayed in fine linen, clean and white: For the fine linen is the righteousness of Saints" (KJV).

This would be grace, the fine linen, and the righteousness of saints is through Christ Jesus. I believe this scripture is speaking of grace. **Revelation 19:9**: "and He saith unto me, write, Blessed are they which are called unto the marriage supper of the Lamb. And he saith unto me, These are the true sayings of God" (KJV). Revelation 19:13–14: "and he was clothed with a vesture dipped in blood, and his name is called The Word of God. And the armies which were in Heaven followed him upon white horses, clothed in fine linen, white and clean" (KJV). In Revelation 19:14 "as the armies" plainly speaks of the church, the bride of Christ, the saints of God. We are one in Spirit as a marriage; we are one in Christ Jesus. This is why we can say by scripture, one God, one Spirit, and one Salvation.

Now, with the knowledge of all scripture shown to me, by what I feel is the Holy Spirit, I will do my best to show you, what I plainly see in scripture. First, remember, these are my thoughts, my understanding, and my opinions of what scripture teaches. Like all religions of the world, they are opinions. Just as each individual reads scripture and sees what he or she believes is truth, I will boldly stand in truth for the Word of God. But, if it be so by God Himself, I will kneel to humbly be corrected. This is what I see!

In my figures, I will use four triangles, but you will notice that only three triangles are colored. Figure B is blue. Figure C is blue and yellow. Figure D is green. For blue with yellow, as one, is green. This is only to symbolize a visual fleshly body, which contains the Holy Spirit. This is only to signify that all four triangles are *one* triangle. This would be the Spiritual body or family of God. The Godhead as figure D. *Stop right there!* Do not start to think this is the same as a three-person God. It is not! Read and study and pay close attention to each scripture. The first triangle, Figure A, is the invisible Spirit of God our Father. The second triangle, Figure B, is the anointed fleshly vessel of God our Father, filled with the same Spirit as found in Figure A. Therefore, the triangles A and B are one in Spirit, symbolically seen as *one* triangle! As far as the vessel or body, Figure B, which is blue, it is a container for figure A, the invisible Almighty Spirit of God our Father. Figure C represents the church, or the Spirit of our Father, the Holy Spirit.

Remember we are *one* in the anointed fleshly vessel of God our Father, known to us as the Son of God, the Son of Man, and the son of David. The anointed flesh vessel of God our Father by name is Jesus the Christ. This is to say, Jesus the fleshly vessel is the Anointed One. Why would this fleshly vessel be the Anointed One? Because it was conceived in the Virgin Mary by the Word of God our Father, the Holy Spirit! Matthew 1:23—read it again in your Bible! This scripture states, "God with us." Well, this means just that! From the anointed flesh vessel of God our Father, we can see His actions and hear His Words taught to us by His anointed fleshly vessel. We cannot see invisible Spirit, Figure A, but we can see and hear flesh, Figure B. Now, Figure B always expresses and shows the action of Figure A. Figure B contains, 100 percent, His Holy Spirit. Now by His actions and words, all sinful flesh can see and hear the Spirit of God our Father, Figure A! Figure B is the fullness with no measure of Figure A (John 3:34). Figure C, the Holy Spirit and the church, are the saints of God. We are as one in Figure A, from the knowledge brought to us in the anointed flesh, which is Figure B, the body of Christ, or anointed fleshly vessel of God our Father, Figure A. The Bible teaches us that, if we believe in Figure B—Jesus, the anointed fleshly vessel of God our Father (1 Timothy 3:16—God manifest in the flesh (KJV)—we are saved through this knowledge. We are the sons and daughters of God; through His Holy Spirit we have received and we have eaten from the tree of life and will live forever (Genesis 3:22).

This is what I believe the scriptures teach. God so loved the world, He sacrificed and gave of Himself, His own anointed flesh vessel, Figure B—the one pure vessel, clean, righteous, innocent of sin, and just! God our Father so loved the world, He crucified His earthly vessel or body in place of our sinful flesh. This is why it is so important for us to know the love and mercy of God our Father, the Almighty invisible Spirit, brought to us by His anointed fleshly vessel, Figure B, known to us as the Son of God, the Son of Man, the son of David, the Anointed One. The Word of God, known to us in flesh in this world as Jesus, the Creator of all. John 1:10: "He was in the world, and the world was made through Him, and the world did not know Him" (NKJV). This, of course, would be His Word, Jesus is the Word of God. One God, one Faith or Spirit, and one Salvation. Jesus the anointed fleshly vessel of God our Father, in the flesh, is the Almighty God. If you will place the spiritual knowledge of Figure A, Figure B, and Figure C inside of one another, you will have, in reality, only *one triangle*, which is Figure D: One God Almighty, one Spirit, the Godhead, the adopted family of God, our Father in Heaven.

The Bible clearly teaches us that there is only one God. This is truth! Figures A, B, and C—the Father, Son, and Holy Spirit—are not three persons or three different entities, or taught as three Gods in one Almighty God. Figures A, B, and C are Almighty God, one Spirit. That one Spirit came to us in the form of man, in the anointed flesh. Why? So we, as flesh, could know Him in the Spirit. He came as man, but perfect and sinless, and offered His pure flesh vessel, clean and righteous, in place of our sinful flesh. God so loved the world that He created that He came into His created world to live a perfect life as man—for humankind.

Think now deeply, and realize that God created us, and He gave us free will. He created us with all of the desires of the flesh. If God had not come as man, how then could we have known Him intimately in the Spirit? When God Himself came to us as man, He brought us the knowledge of who He is by the words He spoke and the actions of His anointed fleshly vessel, Jesus! By the life of Jesus, we now intimately could know God Almighty as the Spirit that He is. By the life, death, burial, and resurrection of Jesus, the anointed fleshly vessel of God, the Almighty Spirit, if we believe in Him, we shall be saved. We will then become heirs with Christ, and receive His Spirit, and become one in Christ, as Christ is one in Jehovah God, our Father. We will now know God Almighty as God our Father in Heaven.

To understand what God our Father has done for us is to know that Jesus, the Son of God, the Son of Man, the son of David, was indeed the anointed fleshly vessel of God Himself. This would be to understand the words we read—Almighty God, all-merciful God, all-loving God, all-knowing God, God, the creator of all, the Almighty! What God our Father has demonstrated by the unmerciful death of Jesus Christ, His pure and clean anointed fleshly vessel, was the ultimate of love. He did this for a sinful world, a world that lived only to fulfill the desires of its sinful flesh. But now, after the life, death, burial, and resurrection of Jesus Christ, if we believe, we will live forever in the Spirit of God our Savior as God intended before the fall of Adam and Eve.

This is an Almighty God. This is an awesome God—the Creator of all things. This is my Father in Heaven, whom I know from the life, death, burial, and resurrection of Jesus the Christ, His anointed earthly vessel. He is my teacher, my mediator, my Savior, my Father in His Almighty Spirit. I am one in Spirit with Christ, as Christ is one in the Father. The truth of God our Father is Spirit. His Spirit is life eternal.

In the final dispensation of time as eternity, we will be in physical sight as spiritual bodies. These bodies will be the same as Jesus after His death, burial, and resurrection as He plainly showed Himself to His disciples. Our Spirits at that time will be united as one with our Father God. Note: The colors in the figures are not as fact; they are only symbolic for an explanation of how I see, or understand, scripture.

One God!

One Spirit!

One Salvation!

One Lord! = FATHER or Christ

One Faith! = CHRIST (and nothing else)

One Baptism! = HOLY SPIRIT or

Christ (and nothing else)

Praise be to God!

ALL IN ALL

The Godhead as I see it

The Godhead as I see it, Figure A

All things are completed with God

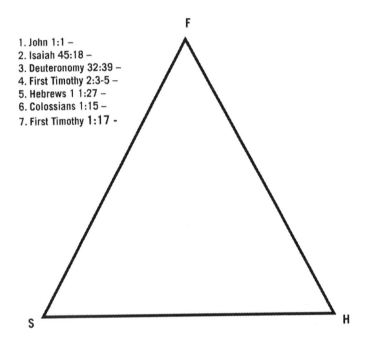

1. John 1:1 –
2. Isaiah 45:18 –
3. Deuteronomy 32:39 –
4. First Timothy 2:3-5 –
5. Hebrews 1 1:27 –
6. Colossians 1:15 –
7. First Timothy 1:17 -

F

S   H

Figure A is Almighty God, He is Invisible Spirit, put this in your mind! You may see Figure A as it is here. But according to the Bible, the Spirit of Almighty God is Invisible!

Praise be to God

The Godhead as I see it, Figure B

All things are complete with God

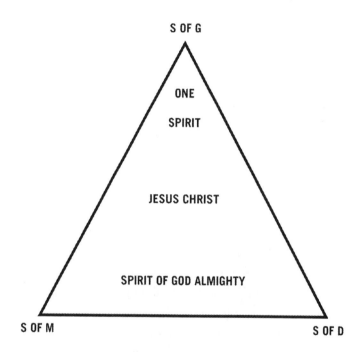

Figure B is visible. This is the reason I have symbolically colored it blue. You can see and hear the flesh of Christ. Put this in your mind!

Praise be to God

Jesus was the Son of God. He was created by the Almighty invisible Spirit. This knowledge is known from the scripture of Luke 1:35 of the King James Version, which reads, "And the angel answered and said unto her, The Holy Ghost shall come upon thee, and the power of the Highest shall overshadow thee: therefore also that Holy thing which shall be borne of thee shall be called the son of God." Note that "Holy thing" in this scripture, I believe, is the anointed vessel of the invisible Spirit, Almighty God. The scripture also reads, "shall be called the Son of God." Think about this strongly! Why would the scripture read "Holy *thing* which shall be borne of thee"? Mary was going to have a child, a son. Why doesn't the scripture state this fact, rather than call the baby a "Holy thing"? Then read, "shall be *called* the Son of God."

By all scripture in the Bible, I believe Jesus was the anointed earthly vessel of God Himself. How can I say this? Matthew 1:23: "Behold, the virgin shall be with child, and bear a Son, and they shall call His name Immanuel, which is translated, God with us" (NKJV). If God is Almighty, surely it is His Word. If God is invisible Spirit in the anointed earthly vessel, this vessel would be known as the Word of God. Read John 3:34 in any Bible. Then read 1 Timothy 3:16: "And without controversy great is the mystery of godliness: God was manifest in the flesh, Justified in the Spirit, seen by angels, Preached among the Gentiles, Believed on in the world, Received up in glory" (NKJV). Now it doesn't matter if the pronoun "He" or the word "God" is used. The scripture is speaking of the Word. Now read John 1:14: "And the Word became flesh and dwelt among us, [this, of course, would be Jesus] and we beheld His glory, the glory as of the only begotten of the Father, full of grace and truth. (NKJV). Now whose glory? I see it as the Father's glory, because it says, the glory "as of "the only begotten of the Father. The Bible teaches me Jesus the flesh man contained the fullness, this is with no measure, of the Holy Spirit our Father in Heaven. In my opinion this is what scripture is telling me. Jesus the flesh man in the world showed us the identity of the Almighty Holy Spirit, the Word of God. How? The word was made flesh and dwelt among us, "As of"---- the Son of God. Note that the "Holy thing" the Bible speaks of literally shows us, the Glory of the Holy Father Himself. We cannot see Spirit, but we can see His only anointed, begotten vessel, called the Son of God.

It may be helpful for you to read these scriptures:

- Colossians 1:15–22
- Hebrews 11:24–27
- 1 Timothy 2:3–5
- Colossians 2:9
- Matthew 1:23
- John 3:34
- John 1:1
- John 1:10
- John 10:30
- John 12:44–45
- John 17:22
- John 13:31
- John 1:14
- 1 Timothy 3:16
- Isaiah 9:6

Here is my opinion of the scriptures, starting with Colossians 1:15–22. (15) clearly states that Jesus was the image of the invisible God. (16) tells me that the pronoun *Him* clearly refers to Jesus. (21) confirms (20), it plainly tells me we once were sinners, as the spirit of this world, but now we have salvation. We are saved, or reconciled, through the Spirit of Christ, which is the Holy Spirit of God our Father—if we believe! (22) reads, "In the body of His flesh through death"(NKJV). Whose flesh? Why, of course, the flesh of God Almighty "to present you Holy, and blameless, and above reproach in His sight." Again, the pronoun *His* refers to the Almighty invisible Spirit, God our Father.

Hebrews 11:24–28: These scriptures simply tell me that we are saved by faith and nothing else. Comparing scripture with scripture, we can see the backbone of our Christian faith, which stems from the knowledge of a Jewish religion.

1 Timothy 2:3–5: (3) simply states truth—God is our Savior. (4) Simply states truth. What we sometimes fail to realize is that the anointed fleshly vessel of Jesus is our knowledge of truth. (5) Simply states truth, as it reads, "the man Christ Jesus" (NKJV). This is not to insinuate two separate persons or entities. The title *Christ* is used first, because Jesus, the fleshly vessel, or *man*, is the anointed Holy Spirit of God our Father, the Christ! The name Jesus is used second because He is the created fleshly vessel of God our Father. The fleshly vessel was man; His name was Jesus. But the word *mediator* helps us understand that this man, or fleshly vessel, Jesus, brought us the knowledge of our Father, because Christ Jesus was God our Father in the fullness of His Holy Spirit. Therefore, Jesus was called by the Word of

God as mediator. Therefore, by hearing the words of Jesus, our mediator, we can know and understand the Almighty invisible Spirit, God our Father. Then by hearing, then by faith, we are saved. Christ our Savior, God our Savior. One in the same—one Spirit, one faith, one salvation, Jehovah God our Savior! Jesus, the name above all names—King of kings, Lord of lords, God Almighty.

Colossians 2:9: This simply tells me that Jesus, the anointed fleshly vessel known as the Son of God, contained all the fullness of God our Father in Heaven. Think about this! On this planet Earth, we are all body, or flesh and spirit. So was God our Father when He came to His creation for our salvation.

Matthew 1:23: This simply tells me that God has come into the world as body and Spirit for our salvation. This scripture states the specific knowledge that God is with us.

John 3:34: The King James Version reads, "For he whom God has sent speaketh the Words of God: [This, of course, is the anointed flesh vessel of Jesus.] for God giveth not the Spirit by measure unto him." This could mean only one thing: the anointed fleshly vessel Jesus contained 100 percent the Spirit of God our Father.

John 1:1: This simply tells me that, in the beginning was the Word, which is God our Father. The Word was with God. Here, the word *with* does not mean "alongside of." To my understanding, it means "together as one." As an example, blue *with* yellow makes, and is green. Therefore, the Word was God. Who was known as the Word of God in the world? Why, of course, Jesus! No Word, no God. If God is Almighty, and He is, then surely it is His Word.

John 1:10: This scripture plainly backs up other scripture, such as Matthew 1:23, 1 Timothy 3:16, John 1:14. Read these scriptures in your Bible. Read more, if you can find them.

John 10:30: The King James Version reads, "I and my Father are one." This scripture should be self-explanatory.

John 12:44–45: (44) tells me, if we believe in that earthly anointed vessel, Jesus, you are believing in the Holy Spirit, our Father in Heaven. (45) tells me, when we see the actions of Christ, we are actually seeing the actions of the Holy Spirit, our Father. This is why Jesus is called the Word of God, or the Holy Spirit. He is both, as He is the Spirit of God our Father, not three persons equaling one God, but one Almighty God in three understandings of the Godhead.

John 17:22: Read this scripture in your Bible. This scripture tells me that Jesus is the Spirit of God. We are of the Spirit of Christ. We are in Christ, as Christ is in the Father—one Spirit. Remember, the body is nothing but a container. Your true identity is your Spirit. Your body will die and rot a way, but your Spirit in Christ lives on forever.

John 13:31–32: Read these verses in your Bible. I believe these verses plainly tell me that the anointed fleshly vessel of Jesus glorifies the Spirit of Almighty God by fulfilling scripture. Remember, Jesus was a fleshly vessel, or the Son of God, but contained the fullness of His Holy Spirit. We are flesh and spirit on this planet, so was God, with anointed flesh, and His Holy Spirit!

John 1:14: "And the Word was made flesh, and dwelt among us" (KJV). This scripture is self-explanatory!

1 Timothy 3:16: Read this scripture in your Bible. The King James Version reads, "God was manifest in the flesh." In the New World Translation it reads, "He was manifest in the flesh." This is rightfully so. This scripture is plainly speaking of Jesus, but without the word *God*, where is the mystery of godliness? The pronoun *He*, in reference to Jesus, is a known fact throughout the whole Bible. We know He is the Word made flesh. What some of us don't know is that the Word is God. No Word, no God!

Isaiah 9:6: The King James Version reads, "For unto us a child is born, unto us a son is given: and the government shall be upon his shoulder: and his name shall be called Wonderful, Counselor, The mighty God, The everlasting Father, The Prince of Peace." Well, now, what is this scripture telling us? The way I see it, the child is Jesus. The son given is the anointed fleshly vessel of Christ, sacrificed for our salvation. He is our Savior. The government upon His shoulder refers to the fact that He is all authority, King of kings. He shall be called Wonderful, Counselor, because He is the Holy Spirit. If He is the Holy Spirit, it is to say He is the Mighty God, the everlasting Father, The Prince of Peace." Which is in one: Father, Son, and Holy Spirit. All one Spirit. All in all!

The Godhead as I see it, Figure C

All things are complete with God

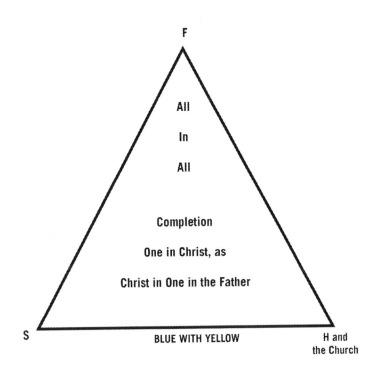

F

All

In

All

Completion

One in Christ, as

Christ in One in the Father

S

BLUE WITH YELLOW

H and
the Church

Figure C, is the Holy Spirit of God, that dwells in Jesus the anointed earthly vessel, with no measures as John 3:34 states. We received the gift of the Holy Spirit from Jesus, which is knowledge of our Father in Heaven, and salvation through Christ. This is symbolically Figure B, which is blue, together with symbolically colored C, as the church yellow, to equal symbolically colored green, which is Figure D. Which is to say, One Spirit, or we say, born-again, this is freely given to us who believe. We now become heirs with Christ. We receive the inheritance, because we are now an adopted child of God. This would mean we are One Spirit, all in all. The Holy Spirit of course is invisible. Because it is the Almighty Power as Spirit, of our Father in Heaven. We cannot see Spirit. We as the church now are visible. But, it is the Spirit I am speaking of. Figure D will show us who we are in Christ. For Christ, as anointed flesh was visible, as we are in this world, body and Spirit.

Praise be to God

This is to simply say that God Almighty on planet Earth was anointed body and Spirit—Jesus the Christ. How can I say this? Matthew 1:23, 1 Timothy 3:16, John 1:10, John 10:30. These are just a few scriptures. Read them in your Bible. There are many more!

If we are all one in Christ, Christ is one in the Father. Then remember the scriptures. The Father is the Almighty invisible Spirit. Christ was that Spirit in the anointed flesh, 100 percent. We are not 100 percent as Christ in the flesh. But through Christ, we are seen by the Almighty Spirit as Father, as 100 percent. Also remember scripture! Christ, the earthly vessel, the Son of God, the Almighty's anointed earthly vessel, was in reality God our Father. How can I say this? Just read one scripture: Isaiah 9:6.

Here are a number of scriptures that explain Figure C.

- Romans 16:25: "Now to Him who is able to establish you according to my gospel and the preaching of Jesus Christ, according to the revelation of the mystery kept secret since the world began" (NKJV). This, of course is the Church Age, the Age of Grace, the saints of God.

- 2 Timothy 1:9: "Who hast saved us, and called us with an Holy calling, not according to our works, but according to his own purpose and Grace, which was given us in Christ Jesus before the world began" (KJV). Did you hear that? Before the world began, our Father knew us before the beginning. What is meant by *us*? The church, the body of Christ, one in the Holy Spirit, the saints of God.

- Romans 8:30: "Moreover whom He did predestinate, these He also called; whom He called, these He also justified; and whom He justified, these He also Glorified" (NKJV). I see this scripture as such. Whom He called, and did come, He justified. This was known to the Father before it happened. This is why the scripture uses the word *predestinate*. It is simply known to the Father, not to us. God does not create some for damnation and some for His Glory. It is strictly our choice. You might ask, what is the purpose for those who will not choose the Spirit of God? Why were they even born into this world? Remember this, we did not ask to be born into *His* world. The gift of life was free for all. The gift of eternal life is also free for all, if we believe! The

Bible teaches us that life-giving rain falls on the just and the unjust. The Bible teaches us that the tares [a weed plant] will grow also with the wheat; this is to say, the saints of God will live in the world alongside the souls that are lost. We who believe are the saints of God, the church, the heirs of Christ, one Spirit, all in all. Remember this also—there has to be an opposite before a choice can be made.

- Ephesians 1:4–5: "According as he has chosen us in him before the foundation of the world, that we should be Holy and without blame before him in love: Having predestinated us unto the adoption of children by Je'sus Christ to himself [*Himself* is the Almighty Spirit God our Father], according to the good pleasure of his will" (KJV). This refers to the church, the saints of God. Remember, He has chosen us only because we have come to Him through the knowledge of Christ. This, for some, may be even in the last hours of life as we know it. He has predestinated us only because no one can take us from His hand.

- 1 Corinthians 6:11: "And such were some of you: but ye are washed, but ye are sanctified, but ye are justified in the name of the Lord Jesus, and by the Spirit of our God" (KJV). This plainly tells me that Jesus is the Spirit of our Father God, and we are in that Spirit. We have been adopted into His family, which is His Spirit. We are one in Christ, as Christ is one in the Father.

- 1 Corinthians 2:16: "For who hath known the mind of the Lord, that he may instruct him? But we have the mind of Christ" (KJV). Who are we? The Church Age saints. A saint is anyone on planet Earth who believes in Christ Jesus, the Word of God.

- 1 Corinthians 3:16: "know ye not that ye are the temple of God, and that the Spirit of God dwelleth in you" (KJV). This, of course, would be the church, the saints of God.

- 1 Corinthians 1:10: "Now I beseech you, brethren, by the name of our Lord Jesus Christ, that ye all speak the same thing, and that there be no divisions among you; but that ye be perfectly joined together in the same mind and in the same judgment" (KJV). This, of course, is the church in agreement of understanding of the Word of God. This, today as well as then, is not going to happen. I believe this is why Paul says, "I beseech you." All things in the world are not perfect. We are not perfect. But the church, the body of Christ, is seen as perfect to our Father God. Why? Because the anointed flesh body of Christ was perfect, and we are in Christ, the body of Christ, the church.

- 1 Corinthians 2:7: "But we speak the wisdom of God in a mystery, even the hidden wisdom, which God ordained before the world unto our glory" (KJV). Whose glory? The glory of the Church Age saints!

- 1 Corinthians 2:13: "Which things also we speak, not in the words which man's wisdom teaches, [this could also mean a religious doctrine] but which the Holy Ghost teaches; comparing spiritual things with spiritual" (KJV). A spirit-filled Christian will discern all scripture with a spiritual mind, not the fleshly carnal mind.

- 1 Corinthians 6:15–17: "know ye not that your bodies are the members of Christ? shall I then take the members of Christ, and make them the members of an harlot? God forbid. what? know ye not that he which is joined to an harlot is one body? for two, saith he, shall be one flesh. But he that is joined unto the Lord is one Spirit" (KJV). This is one in Christ, as Christ is one in the Father—one Spirit, the church as the expression of the Holy Spirit of God in the world today.

- 1 Corinthians 8:6: "But to us there is but One God, the Father, of whom are all things, and we in him; and one Lord Je'sus Christ, by whom are all things, and we by him" (KJV). This refers to the church, the saints of God, as the expression of the Holy Spirit in the world today.

- 1 Corinthians 12:12–14: "For as the body is one, and hath many members, and all the members of that one body, being many, are one body; so also is Christ. For by one Spirit, are we all baptized into one body, whether we be Jew or Gen'tile, whether we be bound or free; and have been all made to drink into one Spirit. For the body is not one member, but many" (KJV). This refers to the church, the saints of God, the expression of the Holy Spirit in the world today.

- John 17:22: "And the glory which thou givest me I have given them; that they may be One, even as we are one:" (KJV). What is the glory our Father has given the anointed fleshly vessel, Jesus? Why, of course, the fullness of the invisible Father's Holy Spirit. Remember, Jesus was a fleshly anointed vessel. We are fleshly vessels, although not perfect anointed vessels as Christ was. But, being of the Holy Spirit, we are seen by the Holy Spirit as perfect. Why? Simply because we believe in Christ Jesus our Savior, and He was perfect. We are all one in Christ, as Christ is one in the Father.

The Father, the son, the Holy Spirit, and the Church Age saints are all one in Spirit. Do you remember the scripture? This was all known to our Father in Heaven before the foundation of the world. In the foreknowledge of God, He has taken the created fleshly man and made him in the image of His Holy Spirit. In the foreknowledge of God before the foundation of the world, the saints of God are in the knowledge of God. This is why He says, "let us make man [create man] in Our Image." Read the book of Genesis again. When you get to Genesis 3:22, read carefully.

This all, of course, is my opinion of scripture. The world is full of opinions—opinions of many religions, Christians, and others. It does not matter what religion, or what kind of religion these opinions come from; they are all opinions—opinions about God, the beliefs about God or gods. The Bible is the Word of God. If you are not a Christian, you may disagree. This would be your opinion. But if you understood and read the Bible, you will see the truth of its teachings. It may seem to some that the Bible contains contradictions in many scriptures, but there are no contradictions. It is all to be understood by understanding all scripture. If you think my opinion of John 17:22 is off base, then I suggest you read the whole chapter of John 17. If you have any spiritual knowledge of scripture, I am quite sure you will see my point. But, again I say, this is merely my opinion.

The Godhead as I see it, Figure D

All things are complete with God

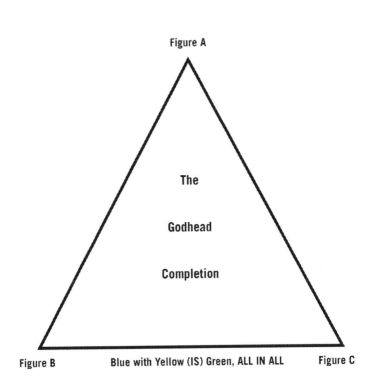

Figure A

The

Godhead

Completion

Figure B   Blue with Yellow (IS) Green, ALL IN ALL   **Figure C**

All three triangles represent the One, and only One triangle, or Spirit in fact, which is the Spirit of God our Father. We as the church are in Him as One Spirit, because of the love He is.

Praise be to God

"Let us make man in our image." This statement was made with the foreknowledge of God Almighty. If this is too much for your mind to comprehend? Then start studying scripture! "Seek me diligently" is what our Father shouts!

Remember, Jesus lived the life we cannot live. He died the death we should die. He did this for us, when we were yet in a rebellious life of sin. This is the Almighty love of God our Savior (1 Timothy 2:3).

Remember, Almighty God, God Jehovah, our Father of Heaven, is the creator of all things. Think about this very deeply, keeping the knowledge of all scripture as billboards in your mind. Look at scripture, and try to understand what I am going to say. If God Almighty is the creator of all things, Heaven and Earth, and all with in them, then He—and only He—is responsible for all things.

If the world had not been created with good and evil, how then could humankind have the opportunity to choose the love of the creator, or the love of creation itself? The love of creation would be the lust of life in this world. If humankind had not had the opportunity to know God, either from the prophets or from Jesus the Christ, how then could we choose?

Before the birth of Christ, humankind received the knowledge of God the Holy Spirit from the relayed messages of the prophets. In that dispensation, the prophets came from among His chosen people, the Jews. It was only Jews who received this awareness of the Almighty Creator. The Jewish religion provided, from the knowledge of the prophets, which came from God, the established faith in the only one and true God, God Jehovah. This was God's responsibility! Why? God Almighty was the creator of good and evil. Again, why good and evil? Without the opposites, there could be no opportunity to decide between loving God our Father the Creator, or giving in to the lust of His creation.

By the birth of the Jewish religion, the will of God for that dispensation, Jews could now live by faith in the knowledge of God. But did they truly know God? Did they truly have an intimate relationship with God as the Holy Spirit as Father? Did any Jew, other than a prophet, or forefather such as Abraham, Isaac, Jacob, or others who had a role in the foundation of the Jewish faith, such as Moses, hear the voice of God? I think not! Jewish people as a whole lived by faith from the knowledge given to the prophets. This truly would be a strong faith.

We, as Christians in this unique dispensation of the Church Age, have His Spirit dwelling in us. If we seek Him diligently, then listen for His voice, He will constantly speak to us through His Spirit. This is justly so, because we are His adopted children. You may ask how I can say this. Let's just take a look at some scripture. Read John 4:21–24. Verse 21 reads, "Je'sus saith unto her, Woman, believe me, the hour cometh, when ye shall neither in this mountain, nor yet at Jeru'sa-lem, worship the Father" (KJV). This scriptures plainly tells me that it is not where we go to worship that it is important. Verse 22 reads, "ye worship ye know not what: [speaking of the Gentiles, for the woman was a Gentile] we know what we worship: for salvation is of the Jews" (KJV).

This, of course, is only because the knowledge of Almighty God was given to the Jew, and only the Jew. This scripture plainly tells me that the Jewish people as a whole knew of God, but even though they did not personally know God, they did have faith. Then, from the bloodlines of the Jewish people, we would receive our Savior, a personal relationship. Verse 23 reads, "But the hour cometh, and now is [Note that Jesus, the Spirit of God our Father, is now on plant Earth] when the true worshipers shall worship the Father in spirit and in truth, for the Father seekth such to worship him" (KJV). In this scripture, Jesus is plainly speaking of a past knowledge of worship, to the present—personal knowledge through Him. Why do I say through Him? Because Jesus is the Word of God. By all the Words He spoke and actions of His life, we, as a whole people, Jew and Gentile, could know the Father intimately. In the next verse, Jesus is also speaking of the future. The truth of this verse would come only after the death, burial, and resurrection of Jesus. Why? Because only after his resurrection could we possibly receive His Holy Spirit. This began two thousand years ago in what is known as the Church Age, or Age of Grace. We who have received His Spirit are the church, the saints of God. We need not necessarily go to a place, or a building of worship to worship Him. Why? Because now His Spirit dwells in us. Our bodies are the temples of the Lord.

This next verse I am speaking of is John 4:24, which reads, "God is Spirit: and they that worship him must worship him in spirit and in truth" (KJV). We are one in Christ; this would mean Spirit. As Christ is one in the Father, this would mean Spirit. Jesus was an anointed earthly vessel filled with the fullness of God. We are earthly vessels filled with the Spirit of Christ. What do the scriptures teach us? In the body of Christ, there are many members. This, of course, would be the church, the saints of God. In these members, which are many, the Bible teaches us that, no matter how great or small, we are all one in Spirit. The Church Age is a very unique and special dispensation of time. Never before the resurrection of Christ did this exist. What am I saying? Never before Christ was the knowledge of God in humankind. Notice that I said, in humankind. Humankind did have knowledge of God, but did not truly know Him before the life of Christ. This is why Jesus says in John 10:30, "I and my Father are one" (KJV). We all could now know Him through His anointed earthly vessel, Jesus the Christ. We now could worship Him in spirit and in truth. How can I say this? John 18:37–38 reads, "Pi'late therefore said unto him, Art thou a King then? Je'sus answered, Thou sayest that I am a king. To this end was I born, and for this cause came I into the world, that I should bear witness unto the Truth. Every one that is of the Truth heareth my voice" (KJV). Look at what Jesus is saying here. He is simply saying that the reason He was born was to show the world, by His existence in the world, the truth of who the Father is. The next verse, verse 38, reads, "Pi'late saith unto him, What is truth? And when he had said this, he went out again unto the Jews, and saith unto them, I find in him no fault at all" (KJV). Look at the significance of these three little words, "what is truth." Remember, the truth of who God is in Spirit was not yet revealed unto humankind. When Pilate said "what is truth," he did not know he was looking face to face with truth. Through the life, death, burial, and resurrection of Christ, we the Church Age saints could now worship Him in spirit and in truth.

Let's take a look at a few more scriptures. John 14:6 reads, "Jesus said unto him, I am the way, the Truth, and the Life. No man comes to the Father except Me" (NKJV). This scripture is often understood to mean that our salvation comes only through Christ. This is rightfully so, especially for the Church Age saints. The Old Testament saints, the Jews, did not know Christ as we do. But they did know of the coming Messiah from the words of the prophets. Even so, they did not know the mystery of the church. The glory of God's church was not revealed until the preaching of Paul, our Grace Age apostle.

So now, with all this said, what else is Jesus telling us? Well, let's just read John 14:7 and find out: "If you had known Me, you would have known My Father also; and from now on you know Him, and have seen Him" (NKJV). Did you hear those words? This scripture plainly tells me that Jesus is the Father in human form. In the last part of that scripture, Jesus is telling me that, from now on, you should know Him because of His life here on planet Earth. Why? Because you have seen Him by the words and actions of His (God's) fleshly vessel. This would plainly explain why Jesus says, "I am the way, the truth and the life."

John 14:17 reads, "Even the Spirit of truth; whom the world cannot receive, because it seeth him not, neither knoweth him: but ye know him; for He dwelleth with you, and shall be in you" (KJV). Look at this scripture closely. Jesus is speaking with His disciples. He tells them that the world cannot receive the Spirit of truth. Then He says, but you know Him, because He lives with you (on planet Earth). But then He says that the Spirit shall be in you. Notice the last line of scripture: "and shall be in you." This is a statement by Jesus in reference to the future. Remember, the disciples knew nothing of the Holy Spirit at this time. Jesus said, if he must go, he would send a comforter. Remember, Jesus was the Holy Spirit in the world. Jesus was the Spirit of Truth. When He left planet Earth, the New Testament came into existence. From the teachings of Paul, by revelation from Christ, we who believe will receive the gift of the Holy Spirit. The Holy Spirit will dwell in us as the church, the saints of God. Now that we are the temples of the Holy Spirit, the Spirit of truth will yet live in the world. We are now in Christ, as Christ is in the Father—one Spirit. From the Spirit of Christ, the teachings of Paul by revelation from Christ, we the church, the saints of God, the body of Christ, *we are* the expression of the Holy Spirit in the world today.

Remember, faith comes by hearing, and hearing comes from the Word of God. Who will preach or teach the Word of God for those to hear in the world today? The church, the saints of God! We will express the Word of God!

I believe God is not in Haven pointing a finger and saying to you—one out of ten people—"I am calling you. The rest of you walk on in your sinful way of life." Everyone in the world, and especially in this country, has the chance to hear the Word of God. It is preached by the Holy Spirit, through man, which comes to man, through Christ Jesus, who was man. We are one in Christ, as Christ is one in the Father. Remember Colossians 2:9 and John 3:34, which speak of

Jesus, the anointed earthly vessel, containing the fullness of the Godhead which is no measure. Well, we are all in Christ, as Christ is all in all, the Holy Spirit of Almighty God. If this is fact, which I believe it is, then we, the church, the saints of God, are part of that Godhead. As the Father sent Christ, the anointed earthly vessel, the Son of God, the Son of Man, the son of David, Christ has sent us, the church. How can I say this? John 20:21–22: So Jesus said to them again, Peace be to you! As the Father has sent Me, I also send you. And when He had said this, He breathed on them, and said to them, Receive the Holy Spirit" (NKJV).

Praise be to God.

The Wonder of It All

Did you ever stop to think, *Why, am I here? Why am I a creation of the Almighty God? For what purpose did He create me? Why is life in this world so hard, but yet so precious in value that we will fight for it? Why do some of us live a much more pleasurable life in the land in which we live while others have little and suffer many hardships in the land in which they dwell? Why are some of us so gifted with talent, wisdom, wealth, and honor while others lack talent, wisdom, wealth, and never receive honor?*

Did you ever stop to think, *Why, are there opposites?* On or off, right or left, go or stop, light or darkness, good or evil. These, as well as many more, are opposites. These opposites are somewhat simple and insignificant in our thoughts as we read them. But in the format of life, at the crossroads of decisions we face as we walk through our journey, some opposites can be critical. If we make a decision to take one path or the other, we have made a choice. This, of course, is free will. Sometimes the choice we make will not affect only us, but others as well. If a person is in the position of what should be an honor, to lead or govern over the people or country, this person will make choices for all. One's decisions may increase or decrease the wealth or honor of their nation. Through history, some men or women have greatly abused this honor.

Did you ever wonder why we have so many great catastrophic events in this world that would take the lives of many innocent people at once, such as earthquakes, tornadoes, hurricanes, floods, tsunamis, and great brush or forest fires? We often call these catastrophic invents acts of God, or the judgment of God. I cannot say that I can accurately agree with either term. Did you ever wonder why so many innocent people are killed at once in a terrorist attack, such as 9/11? Do you ever think of the thousands of innocent Jews and others who were killed in the Holocaust by the Nazis during World War II? Did you ever wonder why so many Christians have been persecuted or killed in some foreign countries? Do you ever think of how, even in this great country of America, Christians might murder Christians? Yes, of course, it was a few centuries back, in other countries, but even so, it did happen. Could it ever happen here? Well, stop to think. Many were burned at the stake because of their religious beliefs. Today we have our great American Constitution to protect us in our religious beliefs. This is a great protector for each individual in America. We have so many religions and cultures in America today that we need a strong Constitution that will protect each and every one of us Americans.

As Christians in this country of America, we must always use our Christian wisdom to cast a vote. We should never think of our pocketbooks or our personal gain when we vote to place a man or woman in a position of honor, such as president of the United States of America. As Americans—true Americans—we should protect the right of any religion or culture of people who are American citizens. This is the true freedom of America. Did you ever think of your choice—the decision you make as you cast your vote—as a vote for the glory of God, your Father in Heaven? Or do you make your choice for your own gain?

Did you ever wonder why there are so many murders each year in our great cities of America? Why we have so many gangs and gang wars, drive-by shootings, and just plain lack of respect for life? Did you ever wonder why so many of our young people today have no respect for themselves? They show this in the manner in which they dress, speak, and act in public. Do you think it's just a fad, or something adolescents are going through today? For some, this may be so. But you'd better think again, and very deeply on this issue.

Did you ever wonder why even some of our middle-age people will speak loudly and boldly in public with great profanity, and think nothing of it?

Did you ever wonder why, even as Christians, we don't always make the mark? Do you ever wonder how a person who loves the Lord Jesus, and knows His Word, could ever fall to the level of others? Well, the reason is that we, as Christians in the flesh, are at that level. We are all of the flesh, all the same. We, as Christians, are all one in Spirit with Christ, as Christ is one with the Father. All the same Spirit! Does this make us perfect, as a fleshly person, as Christians? *No!* We are all of the flesh and capable of sin. Why? Because we are of a sinful nature, which is the fleshly spirit. This is why I say, when we as Spirit-filled Christians, look into a mirror, we will see our enemy. Your Spirit of Christ is in constant battle with your spirit of flesh. Why?

Because the Spirit of God is dwelling in you, and you are of a sinful nature because of your earthly spirit.

Sin is the answer to all of these questions we ask. You might ask, but what about an innocent infant, born sickly, who dies shortly after birth. What about a young child, suffering and dying of cancer? What about a young Christian family killed in a car accident? What about a young man or woman killed in action in a war he or she did not even want to fight? What about a person killed because of his or her race, and nothing more?

We all know by the teachings of God's Word that He is all loving, all merciful, and all-knowing. He loves every one of us on this planet. I do mean every one of us. So we ask, why does He allow these things to happen? Why doesn't He stop these terrible events and untimely deaths of what we call innocent people? Well, I am not God; neither can I speak for God in truth. But, I will give you my understanding of why, taught to me from the Word of God.

In the beginning, God took total care of Adam and Eve. He provided for their every need. They lived in a pleasant world under God's care. They didn't experience a brutally hot summer or a bitterly cold winter. They didn't know anything about the struggles of life. They lived a pleasant and innocent life before they disobeyed God. When they ate from the forbidden tree of knowledge, they came to know good and evil, just as Satan had predicted. Now with the knowledge of good and evil, they could be like God. This is the same reason Satan was cast out of Heaven. He thought he could be like God to the point that he thought he could be in control of all things. This is like humankind's desire to control the world.

So now, because Adam and Eve had disobeyed God, and Satan had shown himself to be a rebellious angel as well, sin came into the world. It was the will of Satan to destroy the beautiful creation of God—the creation God loves so very much. You might ask, if God is the Almighty One, why did He allow Satan to enter into this world? Well, the way I see it, it's because of His love for us who truly love Him! I know what you might be thinking: *Are you crazy? Why would God allow Satan to enter into His created world and cause millions of innocent people to die?* Well, I'm not crazy, so read, and keep all scripture in mind. First of all, none of us are innocent! That is, innocent of sin. Jesus said, when they called Him a good man, that no one was good, but His Father in Heaven. Note that the eyes of the flesh see only flesh. When Jesus said this, He was in the likeness of sinful flesh, but He knew no sin. He was the Spirit of God the Father. This tells me something! Because of sin, we all deserve to die, because sin leads to death. Now because of a sinful world, where sin is taken so lightly, and with no grief and shame, sin will reign, and so will death. You might ask, but why an infant, why the young child, why the young Christian family, why the young soldier, why a person just because of his or her race?

The way I see it, this life is temporary. This world as we know it is temporary. This world is not our home, whether we live one day or a thousand years. The next life is forever, if we are in Christ Jesus. An infant or a young child who has never willingly committed sin will be with Christ. He has paid in full for all with the cup of His blood, which is our New Testament.

Now, about the statement I made concerning Satan being in the world, and the reason being the love of God. It may be hard to understand where I'm coming from if you have little or no knowledge of God's Word. I will explain it so you will understand. First of all, remember that these are my thoughts, not necessarily the way it is. But also remember, the Word of God is for all to read and study as we seek the truth. It is a choice we make in this life on Earth. Once we pass from this learning period of life, we go on into eternity. We may wonder why we are here, why God created us in the first place. Why did God create Satan? If Satan is the opposite of love, truth, goodness, and all righteousness, why? God, our Father in Heaven, is all love, and all of what Satan is not.

God is the creator of all. Everything that is created comes from within His Holy Spirit. Satan, along with all the angels of Heaven, came from within the Spirit of God. Isaiah 45:5–7:

> "I am the Lord, and there is none else, there
> is no God beside me: I girded thee, though
> thou hast not known me: That they may
> know from the rising of the sun, and from
> the West, that there is none beside me. I am
> the Lord, and there is none else. I form the
> light, and create darkness: I make peace,
> and create evil: I the Lord do all these
> things." (KJV).

Now you may be confused, but think about this. Without the opposite of good, which is evil, how then could we truly know good? How could we appreciate love without the knowledge of hate? Remember this: all things are known to God before they ever exist. Everything we have learned from the Holy Word of God—the Holy Bible—is complete with God. We as flesh are merely learning the completion of God's plan.

Satan, along with all the angels of Heaven, were created by God, the Spirit of love. I believe when Satan and many angels of Heaven fell, as we say, maybe it was not because of hate for God, but because of envy. Remember, God created them before he created humankind, and in His presence. They were in Heaven with God. They were also created above humankind, as they were supernatural beings. This makes me think, and very deeply! Think about this: the angels were in Heaven when God our Father created the world, the universe, and humankind. The angels saw the glory of God in His creation and knew it was the apple of His eye. The angels saw and knew the love God our Father had for the world and the creation of humankind. Could this have triggered jealousy toward humankind and envy toward God? Perhaps so. We as humans are taught not to have these feelings grow in us.

Now remember, God knows all things before they ever happen. God knew of the fall of Satan and his band of angels. Satan thought he could destroy humankind and the world, the apple of God's eye, but we must remember that God is all- knowing, and one step ahead. God used the fall of Satan for His plan. Satan may have thought he could destroy the love of God, but by his attempt in the world, Satan caused the format that brought us to the knowledge of the intimate love of God our Father. In return, God receives the intimate love of humankind, His creation! This is love, not by creation, but by choice.

I believe Adam and Eve did not have a clue of this kind of love, and neither did Satan. I also believe the Old Testament saints could not have known this intimate love either. Why? It was not brought to humankind until the life, death, burial, and resurrection of Jesus the Christ. Remember, Jesus was in this world as the Spirit of love, the Spirit of truth, the Spirit of knowledge, and the Spirit of life. He was brought to a sinful and dying world. This is an Almighty God. This was the plan of God. Humankind could now choose the love of God, or the love of this world. This would be a choice. Do we love the creation or the Creator? If our lust for life is greater than our love for the Word of God, which is God, then God may have no part of us. Remember, it is a choice. But if we learn God's Word, we will share an intimate relationship of love with our creator, God our Father in Heaven.

Satan and all the angels did not have this opportunity to choose. They were created in Heaven. They did not experience, in the beginning, a life of lust and sin. They came to know it from the knowledge of good and evil. I believe this is why Satan tempted Adam and Eve to eat from the tree of knowledge. Satan knew that, if they did, they would fall from the grace of God as well. But a righteous God had to give humankind a choice. This is the only way a true existence of love could be intimate in a relationship with the Father, God of creation.

So the answer I offer with regard to why all these terrible things happen in the world is sin! Because of sin, I see the existence of the world as sort of running on autopilot. God can intervene, and sometimes does, but because of sin in the world, there is great sorrow and death. The untimely deaths of Christians, others, or even unborn babies is the result of sin. Do you remember what the Word of God teaches us? This world is temporary! The next is forever, and it will have no sin, no sorrow, and no death. Why? Perhaps because, unlike the angels of Heaven, we have the opportunity to choose and to learn the intimate love of the Father. Perhaps this is why, in our spiritual bodies, in Spirit as one with the Father, we will judge angels. As for now, we are a little lower than angels. But when we get to Heaven in the spiritual form, and receive our inheritance, we will be the apple of God's eye, one in Spirit, and all will be complete in Him, who is all in all!

Praise be to God.

Wake up America

Attention! This is a notice to America, especially our youth of America: Nothing happens unless you make it happen. We are in desperate need of a revival of God's Word, not only in America, but in the entire world.

If you can say you are proud to be an American, then you must realize what it is to be an American. Read the next chapter, "America, a Voice of God." Then keep in mind the word of God and the colors of our flag. In my mind, I can clearly see the red stripes as the blood of our fallen soldiers, the white stripes as the righteous spirit of America, the blue background as the Spirit of God, and the white stars as the many states within her body.

When a body is ill, there is an infection. America is ill! In many of our states, there are many false doctrines of political view. Is your state a falling star in the dullness of its true glory with no brightness of white for the Spirit of God or America? If so, we must pray to our Father God for wisdom and knowledge. We, as Christians of America, the children of God, must pray. We cannot fight physical problems with physical force. We must pray! Ephesians 6:12 teaches us this truth. Go to your Bible and read it for yourself.

Let us not lie down in a slumber, but awaken to the Spirit of God. It is time for a revival of God's Word. Our nation is ill! Wake up, America, or lose your voice. Copy the chapter, "America, a Voice of God." Take it to your pastors, to the leaders of your faith. Post it on Facebook. E-mail it to your friends with a spiritual and national plea. Then, may God bless you, and America!

Praise be to God

America, a Voice of God

After viewing the recently released motion picture *America*, I was inspired in my spirit to express in words what the picture projected. I am a Christian in the Spirit of Christ. I am also an American. America is also in the Spirit of Christ, expressed from our forefathers in the document of our great American Constitution. Today, many of our men and women, with great minds and eager hearts, wish to serve this great nation in leadership. Some may have the mind of Christ in Spirit, and some may not. The voice of America may be weighed on the scales of justice.

I understand that, throughout God's created world, many will disagree. Those who disagree perhaps do not know God's Word, or do not fully understand. If we look at the history of America, then compare it to the Words of God in the Holy Bible, we can see how America is in favor of the Word of God. Therefore, God would be in favor of America.

When the early settlers arrived in America, they brought with them the Geneva Bible. This Bible was an early English translation of scriptures. The brave men and women who traveled to this new land trusted in God. They brought with them the Word of God. No one in this new land had any knowledge of the Word of God.

Let me express these thoughts first: Every great nation on this planet, in my mind, is as of one individual body. Within the body, or nation, there are many members. The people of each nation are what form that body or nation. The Bible teaches us as Christians that we are members of the body of Christ. Now, as each individual person forming the body of Christ, does this make us sinless and perfect? The answer I have is no. Why? Because we are still of the flesh, and the flesh is sinful. But we are also of His Spirit. His Spirit will drive us in the direction of His truth. If we, as flesh, make some great mistake in our judgment in a life matter, but turn to God for guidance, He will lead us in the direction of a positive ending. As Christians, we should always walk in the spirit of truth, which is the knowledge of Christ. If we do this as individuals, or as a nation, there will be less chance of any great mistakes, but as I said, God will make good of any repented evil, or what is seen as evil.

In the history of America, it doesn't matter who came here first, or who was here first. What matters is the reason people came to America. Remember, in the foreknowledge of God, all things are known from start to finish before they ever exist. God had a plan for a great nation of the Western hemisphere; it was America! The history of America and how she became a great nation is not a pretty picture. Many men, women, and children perished in the pursuit of happiness—to dwell in a land where they could freely worship the *one and true God*. This land was already inhabited for centuries by what we call today the American Indians. The Indians of America were many different tribes. These tribes fought amongst themselves for centuries to gain control of the land. As they fought amongst themselves, many men, women, and children perished. Even though the American Indians were, and still are, a very spiritual people, the birth of America brought them the knowledge to worship, in Spirit, *the one and true God.*

The American colonies that settled in America were under British rule. After many years of hard work, the colonies grew in strength. Once they grew with power in numbers as strength, they had enough of the British rule. The colonies were in a land far from Great Britain. They decided to fight for their independence. This, of course, was treason by British law, and clearly seen as such by the rulers of Great Britain. But in the eyes of the colonists, it was the only way to establish their own laws in a new land. The Revolutionary War was fought, and as a result, America was born.

Our forefathers of the revolutionary era had great knowledge of God's Holy Word. It was from this knowledge that our great American Constitution was documented. Did this act of treason and this great American Constitution make America sinless? No, of course not! We are all of the flesh, and the flesh is sinful. Remember this as well—we are of the Spirit of Christ, for America was founded as a Christian nation. America had been born, as a babe in Christ. America would experience the horrors of sin as she fought for additional land. This, of course, was the Indian Wars. Since the beginning of time, once humankind had established a culture or society with power and strength, he would either conquer or be conquered. America was no different in her lust for new land. Did this mean God was not with her? I think not! Remember, America was still a babe in Christ. America had fought her battles for the gain of land; this would also include the Spanish-American War. Many lives were lost on both sides during these battles.

America grew in the wisdom of God's Word. She now would experience the growing pains of a new Christian nation. Though we are a nation of many people from around the globe who embrace different religious beliefs, we are Americans. Our great American Constitution, created in 1787, then ratified in 1788 gives us this freedom of religion and culture. We must also remember it is a Christian value, not to be altered. Our Constitution ensures freedom— liberty and justice for all.

America was clearly divided in the understanding of God's Word. The result? A Civil War. I want you to think very deeply, as a Christian, about what I'm going to say. If you are not a Christian, it may do your soul some good if you will comprehend these words.

First remember this, we are of the natural—flesh and blood. The Bible teaches us that to be born of the natural is to be born with a sinful nature. I was told this once, and it is truth. We are not sinners because we commit sin; we sin because we are sinners. America, as a nation, is filled with thousands upon thousands of sinners; and, not only America, but every continent on this planet. The people on this planet, whether they know it or not, need the Word of God. To know the Word of God is to know how to choose good from evil, right from wrong. The world is a sinful and evil place. Look at the words of Psalms 23:4: "yea, though I walk through the valley of the shadow of death, I will fear no evil: for thou art with me; thy rod and thy staff they comfort me" (KJV). The valley of death is the world, because it is sinful, and sin leads to death. When the scripture says, "thy art with me, thy rod and thy staff they comfort me," I believe the scripture is implying that the power and the wisdom of God is within your Spirit, but only if you are reborn in His Spirit, the image of God.

In the year of 1861, America was still a very young nation. The people of America had fought and won their independence from Great Britain in 1776. The great country of America was only seventy-three years old, as was her great Constitution. Our constitution was complete and a document of law in the year 1788 June 21. Young and foolish are we, as each individual, so was America in her youth. We can truly thank God in this year of 2015 that our forefathers had the wisdom and knowledge of God's Word. Abraham Lincoln was truly a man of God. Even though he was flesh and blood, and capable of sin, and may have had other motives as well, he knew what it meant when the Constitution read, "justice and liberty for all." He knew the voice of God had been heard by the men who drafted our great American Constitution. Abraham Lincoln knew that America had to be a voice of God. Knowing God was with him in the belief of freedom—justice and liberty for all—Abraham Lincoln ruled with a rod of iron and a staff of truth. The bloody Civil War of the United States of America—the North versus the South—was truly a voice of God. Many men of the South may have had a closed ear, or no knowledge of the Word of God. These men were caught up in the birth of a new nation growing swiftly with technology and wealth.

The Bible says the love of money is the root of all evil. Note that it says the *love* of money, not the money itself. Many of God's people were very wealthy, but they put God first.

Many people of the South at this time may have claimed to love God, but did they know Him? For if they did, they would never have embraced slavery. Although slavery has been in the world for over 4,000 years, every race of man a victim at one time or another, and most likely it happened in every continent on this planet, it is not the will of God. We as Americans can thank God for the wisdom and knowledge of our forefathers, Christian people! This is why we can pledge allegiance to America, one nation under God, with liberty and justice for all. America is a voice of God. This is why we say, "God bless America." To my knowledge, America fought a civil war. A war of disagreement within its self. Though other issues, the strongest debate was Federal law verses Individual State law. The Federal Government wanted to abolish slavery. The Northern and Southern states could not come to a civil agreement. This is plainly seen in my eyes as the Spirit of God—of righteousness—in battle with the spirit of the natural man. America is a voice of God. This is why we truly say, "God bless America."

Someone recently said, "God damn America." May God forgive him, as I do. The Bible teaches us to forgive. This is not a benefit to the offender, but a benefit to the victim. If we hold hatred within our hearts, it will blind our eyes and close our ears. We will not see the love of God in the actions of His will; neither will we hear the Words of His wisdom. Psalms 23:1–3: "The Lord is my shepherd; I shall not want. He maketh me to lie down in green pastures: He leadeth me beside the still waters. He restoreth my soul: he leadeth me in the paths of righteousness for his name's sake" (KJV). Do we understand these words? Do we even hear these words? If God were to tell us in plain English what these words mean, we still might not understand, or even hear His words. Study the Bible—the Word of God—to gain wisdom and knowledge in the Spirit of God. This will bring peace within us and peace on Earth.

America, though a Christian nation, a voice of God, has had many bloody conflicts of war, the wages of sin. Many of our great men and women of America have fought bloody wars and died on foreign soil. I pray that the young men and women, many just teenagers—young people who didn't fully understand life, much less the reasons for war—are with our Lord God as voices of victory. The American soldier shouts "liberty and justice for all," even to the death. If this were not the righteous will of God, why would America conquer, and then give back what she conquered, plus give of herself to rebuild what she destroyed? World War I and World War II were not fought by America for gain of power or wealth. Conflicts in Korea, Vietnam, and the Middle East were no different. America fought for justice and liberty, not for the spoils of war. America fights for freedom for all humankind; this is a voice of God, because it is the will of God. America did gain wealth and power, but it was the blessings of God. Socialism and communism are not the will of God. How can I say this? God created us with free will—the will to choose good or evil with His knowledge, the will to fight for good and against evil with His knowledge. The world was created by God. "He is our Father; He is our Savior. He is King of kings and Lord of lords". This of course is my opinion of what I see the words of …Isaiah 9:6 insinuating. This is why justice and liberty will rule in the world. It is the will of God. If the world had evolved as some great, but foolish, minds teach, then the world would be up for grabs for the most dominant to rule. Humankind, with a sinful nature and sinful heart, cannot rule anything for long. How can I say this? Just read history! There have been many empires, many conquerors, and many failures. Humankind without the Spirit of God dwelling in him will not succeed in justice and honor. In the natural world—humankind's world—there will always be a most dominant element that will conquer. To be the most dominant is to be the most lustful being. His lust would be for himself, and no one else. He would be the definition of sin—Satan! Wake up, America, and shout! Be a voice of God once more. Wake up, sleepy Christians! Politics and religion do mix; they do go together. Your knowledge of God is truly not religion; it is relationship, fellowship, your knowledge of the identity of Jesus, and to be with God in Spirit as one! This knowledge comes from His Word—the Holy Bible. If you do not have the knowledge, wisdom, and Spirit of God in you, how then can you vote for anyone and expect it to be in him or her? Wake up, America, or lose your voice of God.

Praise be to God.

P.S. Here's a personal suggestion, with a bit of humor: Put this in your pipe and smoke it. Let it filter into your brain, into your blood, into your heart. Then decide if you are a real American!

Get Down from Your
Holy Pedestal

That may sound harsh, but many of us may place ourselves on a Holy pedestal and point that Holy finger. We may be guilty of judging others. We may not realize we are passing judgment when we disagree with someone's character. I know the Bible teaches we may judge sin. This would be, of course, to know good from evil. To disagree might be the bottom line to pass judgment. I can honestly say I disagree with a lot of things, even some things pertaining to law, such abortion rights set forth by *Roe versus Wade.* If you are a Christian as I am, you should disagree as well, and rightfully so. Why would we disagree? Because God's law is truth; it is just, it is solid, it cannot be moved, it will not change. Sometimes humankind's laws are flexible and will change. Don't get me wrong; I respect humankind's laws—to a certain degree. If humankind's law conflicts with God's law, then I would have to disagree. I know God's law is solid, and it will not change.

In today's society, we have many disagreements as a people of one nation. Disagreement is also the reason for the existence of many Christian religions. Disagreement is also the reason for the existence of many non-Christian religions. Disagreement is also the reason for some organizations that will pass judgment on people only because of their race. Disagreement is the reason many of these issues have led to the bloody fields of war.

We all have a God-given right to disagree. We, as Americans, not only have a God-given right, but a constitutional right as well. It's what we do with this right, in our thoughts, emotions, and actions, that makes a difference. We may legally protest for disagreement, but if we step outside the boundaries of law, we may become lower than the disagreements we protest. I believe people should stand up for their beliefs, but if your actions are not under God's law, or humankind's, you don't have a leg to stand on. As they say, two wrongs don't make it right!

Disagreement, if justified, may fall in the hands of God. Though we live in an evil and sinful world, God is still in control. The bottom line: it is God's decision. The early settlers of America agreed to fight for their independence; British law disagreed with this, seeing it clearly as treason and punishable by death. America, with the Grace of God, won her independence in 1776. Our great American Constitution was written by God-fearing man, with the laws of God in mind. America was founded as a Christian nation. Some Americans, believe it or not, may disagree with this justified disagreement. If so, perhaps they don't have much use for God's law, or His Word. I don't know; I just can't imagine why anyone would disagree with the disagreement that was justified by God. How can I say this? As this has been documented for many years: "I pledge allegiance to the flag of the United States of America, and to the Republic for which it stands, one nation, under God, indivisible, with liberty and justice for all." Freedom! America is the only country to my knowledge that has ever fought against itself to end slavery. Praise be to God! Even after all this is said, some Americans—repeat: Americans—point their finger of so-called justice at the disagreement that the God of Heaven has justified. Some Americans just won't bury that dead beast, put that filth in the ground, and let it rot. Only then will America's soil become rich, with a ray of splendor color.

Here in America we have many social and religious disagreements. Why? Because we are a nation of different races, ethnic backgrounds, and cultural and religious beliefs. As Americans—true Americans—no one has the right to point that justified and so-called Holy finger. According to the First Amendment of our great American Constitution, "Congress shall make no law respecting an establishment of religion, or prohibiting the free exercise thereof; or abridging the freedom of speech, or of the press; or the right of the people peaceably to assemble, and to petition the Government for a redress of grievances." We, all as Americans, Christian or non-Christian, have the right to believe and express our religious beliefs. If we have no religious beliefs and completely rely on the theory of evolution, this is also our freedom of choice, and it also may be expressed. This is what makes America a great nation. The problem is, many Americans forget this great First Amendment of our great American Constitution. God created us, in my belief, and He gave us a free will. The laws of our great American Constitution run parallel to the will of God. God loves every one of us on this planet and gave us all the freedom of choice. We must respect our freedom and the decisions of choice. If any American will make a lawful choice within the law of God and humankind, then maybe we, as Americans, should silently respect that choice.

Bubba

As a Christian, my belief, my freedom, and my will, is that everyone on this planet would come to know the one and true God, Jesus Christ. One Lord = Christ Jesus. One faith = Christ Jesus. One baptism = Christ Jesus.

Now I want you all to pay close attention to my thoughts and my concerns on this subject. I have made this statement a few times in *My Study*: God loves every one of us on this planet, and I do mean every one of us. The book of Acts, chapter 10, verse 34 of the King James Version reads, "Then Peter opened his mouth, and said, Of a truth I perceive that God is no respecter of persons." This scripture, to my understanding, tells me that God shows no favoritism, one person over another. This can mean only one thing, to my understanding. This is that God loves everyone in equal value. Remember that Christ Jesus died for the sins of the world. This, of course, would be every living soul. This also would mean Christians and non-Christians, believers in God or gods, or those who have no beliefs at all. This also would mean heterosexual or homosexual, or any so-called lifestyle. Now don't start to point that Holy finger at me just because I brought this subject up. Many of my Christian brothers and sisters understand that we, by the Word of God, have the right to judge sin, but we all have sin, and we have no right to judge another to the level of condemning them. I know what the scriptures read! Now before you disagree or agree in judgment, remember your decision may place you in the judgment of God, the Creator of all. This, of course, would be Christ Jesus. Look at the words of John 1:10 in the King James Version: "He was in the world, and the world was made by him, and the world knew him not."

This would be God, the Creator of all. This same Christ Jesus—as the teacher to humankind that He was—taught us a very important lesson in the gospel of John 8:3–8:

> "The scribes and Pharisees brought to Him a woman caught in adultery. And when they had set her in the midst, they said to Him, Teacher, this woman was caught in adultery, in the very act. Now Moses, in the law, commanded us that such should be stoned. But what do you say? This, they say, testing Him, that they might have something of which to accuse Him. But Jesus stooped down and wrote on the ground with His finger, as though He did not hear. So when they continued asking Him, He raised Himself up and said to them, He who is without sin among you, let him throw a stone at her first. And again He stooped down and wrote on the ground" (NKJV).

Note that the Bible does not ever say what Jesus wrote on the ground. But, by what knowledge I believe I have, my spiritual guess would be the Ten Commandments. John 8:9–11:

> "Then those who heard it, being convicted by their conscience, went out one by one, beginning with the oldest even to the least. And Jesus was left alone, and the woman standing in the midst. When Jesus had

raised Himself up and saw no one but the
woman, He said to her, woman, where
are those accusers of yours? Has no one
condemned you? She said, "No one, Lord."
And Jesus said to her, neither do I condemn
you; go and sin no more" (NKJV).

Jesus was the only one there who had no sin and could have
condemned her. But what did he tell her? He said, "Neither
do I condemn you; go and sin no more." Now, I want to ask
you something. Do you believe, because Jesus said, "Neither
do I condemn you, go and sin no more" that this woman
would never sin again? Of course not! She is still born of the
natural, with a sinful nature, which in my understanding
is the spirit of the flesh. Jesus was simply telling her go, but
stop living a life of lust of the flesh, but rather to follow Jesus
and His teachings, which is the knowledge of everlasting life.
John 8:12 is my understanding: "Then Jesus spoke to them
again. Saying, I am the light of the world. He who follows me
shall not walk in darkness, but have the light of life" (NKJV).

The Bible teaches us, as it reads in 1 Peter 1:16: "Be ye Holy;
for I am Holy" (KJV). This verse simply tells me that we
must separate ourselves from the cares, or the lust, of this
world. We must simply cut these things away, or as the
Bible teaches, circumcise our hearts from the will of the
flesh. In my opinion the Bible also teaches or insinuates in
Isaiah 64:6: "Our righteousness [holiness] are as filthy rags,
in His sight." Why would the Bible teach us to be Holy as
He is, then say, as a direct contradiction that our holiness
is of a dirty rag in His sight? It makes no difference if we
are a Jew of the Old Testament, or a saint of God in the

New Testament; we are all of a sinful nature. So there is no contradiction; we must simply change our worldly views of life to the knowledge of God. But we must remember who we are in the flesh. We are all sinners. We must never place ourselves as Christians on that Holy pedestal. We are seen as Holy only because of what Christ did for us. His blood covers our sin. If we believe and know this truth, God the Almighty Holy Spirit, our Father will see us as righteous and Holy, as our Redeemer, our Savior Christ Jesus, God's anointed earthly vessel.

If you are a Christian, and someone comes to you for a drink of the Holy Spirit and you refuse, this is not the will of God. Jesus said to His disciples, "When you gave me drink." His disciples replied, "Lord, when did we give you drink?" Jesus answered, "When you have given it to the least of my brothers you have given it to me." Jesus told the woman at the well, "Drink of my water and thirst no more." To deny anyone a drink of the Holy Spirit, in my opinion, is to unjustly judge them. All sin is an abomination, because sin leads to death. We are not gods in this world, but Christ was God, and came to show His love. Christ did not come to condemn the world; he came so that, by His life, all might be saved. We as the church, or saints of God, are the expression of the Holy Spirit in the world today. As Christ we should not condemn, but show His love, that all might be saved.

I heard a preacher—a man I respect very much—say these words, "No one loves God as much as I do." If this is so, praise be to God. But does God love this man any more than He loves you or me? I once heard a preacher say, "I have never had a beer touch my lips, I have never had a cigarette touch my lips, I have never spoke with profanity through my lips." If this is so, praise be to God. But does God love this man any more than He loves you or me? I would think not. Why? The thief on the cross. This man, who was crucified with Christ, defended the righteousness of Christ. The man on the other side of Christ mocked Him. The defender of Christ asked Christ to remember him. Christ replied to the man, "This day you will be with me in paradise." What does this scripture tell me? There is nothing we can do for God, but believe what He has done for us. The thief on the cross may never have even prayed to God. He may never have received water baptism. He may have never have spoken in tongues. But he did receive the gift of the Holy Spirit, which is salvation, the knowledge of God.

These two preachers I spoke of may have a greater knowledge and wisdom in the Word of God than you or I or the thief on the cross. Their knowledge and wisdom may place them at a higher level in the kingdom to come on Earth. For it is written that the saints of God will rule in the kingdom, the saints of God will judge angels. But for now, in this life, as flesh, we are all sinners. We must never place ourselves on a Holy pedestal and point that Holy finger. We sometimes, ignorantly, may chase more people away from God than draw them to Him.

I can honestly say that I don't know all the answers. I can only agree or disagree with the issues of life by the judgment in God's Word. But I do know one thing for sure—that God loves each and every one of us with equal value. He values our souls.

Praise be to God.

Temptation

The sight of a beautiful woman, the thought of a handsome man,

May draw within your spirit, the cards of a willing hand,

Though truth in sight, or thought in mind,

With feelings very real,

Should I fold this hand in righteous Spirit, or play its fateful deal.

Some years back, I went to Atlanta, Georgia, for a Manpower event. This is an event designed to give men knowledge of the inspirational messages of the Word of God. There were many well-known preachers there, preaching the Word of God to strengthen our Spirits in Christ. I went with a friend from work and his church group. We traveled on a school bus, which allowed us to have fellowship and many conversations concerning the Word of God.

On the way back, we stopped at a restaurant to eat. As we sat around the tables in joyful conversation about our trip, I overheard a conversation between two young men seated at the end of the table. They were both probably twenty-something years younger than I. They were deep into their conversation, and I could tell it was quite serious to the both of them. As I listened with eager heart to speak, I chuckled within my spirit. Their conversation was truly not a laughing matter. It only tickled my spirit, because the topic was no surprise to me. Their conversation was about lust.

Now I truly don't remember the exact words I spoke, but they were to this effect: I asked the young man what his deep concerns were in the matter of lust. He said, "You know I love the Lord, and I love His Word. I want to follow Him and live a righteous life, but I have this problem of lust. Every time I see a pretty girl, something happens inside of me. I have these feelings that excite me inside, and I can't help those feelings. I want to look at her again." I said to him, "You mean you have these feelings when you see a jaw-dropping, eye-popping, knockout beautiful woman?" He looked at me with great surprise. Then I quickly asked him, "Are you heterosexual or homosexual?"

The point was, and is, if he were homosexual, then I could understand his concerns. Having these thoughts about a woman would be unnatural to him, and therefore sinful lust. But since he was heterosexual, his concerns were not valid to the sin of lust, because it is a natural feeling God bestowed in his earthly spirit. We can accept these feelings of God's beautiful creation being in sound mind and heart for the Word of God. But we must never defile them with the lust of a sinful heart by taking our thoughts from an appreciation of beauty to a sexual level. This is true to both the homosexual and the heterosexual, because God created each of us from birth the way we are. This, of course, is my opinion; many may disagree.

Temptation is of Satan. He is out to destroy God's beautiful creation in every way. If we do not truly understand who we are in the flesh, then how can we ever understand who we are in the Spirit of Christ? Only when the Spirit of Christ dwells within us can we put the flesh spirit under subjugation.

If you have read my chapter "I Am a Christian" in this little book, *My Study*, you should plainly see that even Christ dealt with temptation. Why would Christ deal with temptation? Because He was a fleshly man with a fleshly spirit, but He did not consider it robbery to be equal with God (Philippians 2:6 in any Bible). Why is it not robbery to be equal with God? Because Christ contained the fullness in Spirit of God, and God is invisible Spirit! This is the only reason Satan could not defeat Christ with temptation. He could not destroy God's plan, or His creation. Why? Because the Spirit of God is greater than the spirit of flesh. Only God can completely conquer the flesh and put it under subjugation. This is an Almighty, all-loving, all-merciful, awesome God.

When we humans of fleshly and earthly spirit accept Christ, we grow strong in His Word and in His Spirit. Christ is the Word and Spirit—which are one—of our Father in Heaven, God Jehovah, proven by John 1:1 and John 3:34 KJV. We too, may place the fleshly spirit under subjugation to the Spirit of Christ, who is the Spirit of God. How can I say this? The Bible teaches that we are all one in Christ, as Christ is one in the Father: All one Spirit. We are not sinless and perfect in this world. Why? Because we are not 100 percent the Spirit of God as Christ was in His earthly ministry. But, through the Spirit of Christ, we are seen blameless and without blemish or spot.

In the everlasting dispensation of time, which we know as eternity, there will be no temptation. Why? It will have been cast into the deepest pits of hell with Satan, its author of deception. At that time, the Church—the saints of God—will be complete in Christ, as Christ is complete in the Father. All in all.

To those with a concerned mind and heart, just remember this: we live in an imperfect world, a world of lust and sin. Because of sin, there are many questions why. Why did God create two babies stuck together at birth? Why was one born in the world blind, never to see the beauty of God's creation? Why was one born to die shortly after birth? Why was one born homosexual? You may disagree! But why? One might say it's a chosen lifestyle. If that is the case, did heterosexuals choose to be attracted to the opposite sex? Or did God create us to be attracted to the opposite sex? As a heterosexual man, I just can't buy that anyone chooses whom they are attracted to. One might say it's an evil spirit of a perverted lustful desire. In our youth, don't we all lust for another at some point in our lives? Well, let's be honest with ourselves. Could we grow old with the youthful lust of desire for a person of the same sex, if we were not created that way? Any monogamous couple that remains together for years and years as they grow old together are not prompted to do so because of an evil spirit or a perverted lustful desire. This type of relationship is always because two individuals have a true love for one another, be it heterosexual or homosexual.

Neither heterosexuals nor homosexuals should flaunt sin to the open view of the world. This is not appreciated by God or humankind. Sinful acts are just that—sinful. To participate in a decadent celebration, or to have a night out with the boys at your local strip club is to flaunt sin. To sit and watch a heartwarming, heartbreaking, tear-jerking movie of a young couple's love story may also flaunt sin. How? I've been told on several occasions, "You have got to watch this movie. It is so good." After viewing the movie, I could not agree. It truly may have been interesting from a fleshly point of view, but in the Spirit of Christ, it was an abomination. Why an abomination? The characters were never married. This would be adultery. This would be sin. Sin leads to death. This is an abomination.

As a heterosexual Christian man, I do not fully understand the life of a homosexual. Why? Because I am heterosexual; that is reason enough. I may not fully agree or disagree with the social needs and lawful desires of a homosexual. Why? Because I truly don't know the answers. But I do know one thing. Christ came into the world not to condemn the world, but so that the world might be saved by Him. Jesus left us as the church, as the Holy Spirit in the world today, not to condemn, but to teach and share His Word, that the world might be saved.

Praise be to God.

Marriage

If you have read my testimony, or have known me quite well, you might think I have no authority to speak on this subject. Honestly, of the flesh, I don't. As a man in the Spirit of Christ, I may not have the authority by world standards, but I do have spiritual knowledge—knowledge given to me from the Word of God. Knowledge that even a pastor or a marriage counselor may not be aware of. I truly don't know.

I am not claiming to know all there is to know for people to have a wonderful marriage. I do know that marriage is two, joined together as one. In the physical realm. I can see marriage as two mules hitched to a wagon. Both are working hard through the struggles of the day. Both are in constant labor to ease the workload of the other. Together they are a massive power. Two well-trained mules together as one have a common goal. This would be to perform in life as to be expected. This, of course, would please their master's wishes. These two mules together as one would justly be rewarded. The master would surely care and tend to their every need.

We humans should compare our thoughts to these dumb animals. First of all, we must be well trained in the knowledge of Christ. Two mules—or two people—joined together as one have a great power. Like the two mules joined together with the knowledge of their master, we humans should be joined together with the knowledge of Christ. This is great power—power enough to accomplish any goal.

The problem with a young mule, or a young human, may be a self-centered attitude. One half of the team may start to feel he or she is pulling a little harder than the other. This may cause one to lack respect for the other. One may slow down in his or her pace, causing more of the workload to shift to the other. This shift may cause a chain reaction, and this, of course, would cause great stress, because they are truly not working together as one. This actually applies to any aspect in life.

The Bible teaches us that we are the brides of Christ, as the church, the saints of God. But we all understand that, in the physical realm, a bride is a female. We as the church, the saints of God, are many members; we are male and female. Even so, we are called the brides of Christ. Why would both males and females be called the brides of Christ? Like a marriage, in Spirit, we are one in Christ, as Christ is one in our Father.

Let's take a look at how the dictionary defines the word *marriage*. The *Webster's New World Dictionary* defines the word as such: "1, the state of being married. 2, the act of marrying; wedding. 3, a close union." Let's also take a look at the word *marry*: "1, to join as husband and wife. 2, to take a husband or wife. 3, to unite." In the physical realm, we can surely see marriage as the union of a man and woman. In the spiritual realm, I can clearly see a marriage as "to be a close union," or "to be united as one." This, of course, is the same as it is to be united in Christ, as Christ is united in the Father, as one Spirit. In the spiritual realm, there is neither male nor female, in the Spirit of Christ, which is the

Spirit of the Father. Our spirits are simply bonded in a close union—or united as one—with the Father, through Christ.

I have been a welder most all of my life. Welders often refer to welding as "marrying" multiple pieces of steel together, making them one. So let's just take a look at the dictionary, and how it defines the word *weld*: "1, to unite pieces of metal, by heating until fused or until soft enough to hammer together. 2, to unite closely, to be welded.3, welding, a joint formed by welding."

Let's also take a look at what the dictionary has to say about the word *bond*: "1, anything that binds, fastens, or unites. 2, shackles. 3, a binding agreement. 4, an obligation imposed by a contract, promise, etc. 5, the status of goods kept in a warehouse until taxes or duties are paid. 6, and interest-bearing certificate issued by a government or business, redeemable on a specified date. 7, surely provided against theft, embezzlement, etc. 8, an amount paid for bail."

In the physical realm, which is life here on planet Earth, a Christian marriage is clearly seen as a celebration, known as Holy matrimony. In this celebration, two are joined together as one, by obligation imposed by a contract or promise. This simply means they are united; they are in a binding agreement. This binding agreement is a marriage certificate issued by the government of the state in which they reside. This also would mean that, in the physical world, two are shackled together, working together as one for a common goal.

In the spiritual realm, I can clearly see the celebration of Holy matrimony as a way for the participants to set themselves apart from the world, joining together with one, and forsaking all others. The two are now joined together as one in flesh and spirit. You might ask, how can I include the spirit in this marriage celebration? First of all, whether you believe this or not, your actions in this physical world of flesh are etched, or embedded, into the spiritual history of your very existence here in this life. This, of course, is a record of your soul. What God has joined together, no one can separate. In the physical realm, this marriage contract may be annulled by a so-called church, or by the legal formalities in a court of law. This truly will not set us free from the spiritual bond. Only Christ is our spiritual redeemer of any bond. Only Christ can pay the bail to redeem us from any spiritual bond. This also would mean any sin caused by the natural fleshly spirit. Christ is our mediator, Christ is our redeemer, Christ is our Savior, Christ is our God. What Christ has joined together, no one can separate.

In the physical realm of flesh and earthly spirit, what any two have willingly joined together is also a bond. This would be a spiritual bond as well. Only Christ can separate this spiritual bond and set us free, allowing us, as Spirit, to be bonded only as one in His Spirit, the Spirit of Christ, the Spirit of Almighty God Jehovah, our Father in Heaven— all one in the same Spirit of our Father in Heaven. In this physical realm of life, if we lie with another in a sexual relationship, we are bonded spiritually forever, whether the union is recognized by a written agreement of a marriage certificate or not! What has come together as flesh has also come together as spirit. Why? We are body and spirit. What is etched in the record of your soul are the actions of your earthly spirit. You think not? Well, let's just see what the Bible has to say.

The first scriptures that come to mind in relation to what I just stated is in John 4:7–18:

> (7) "a woman of Samaria came to draw water. Jesus said to her, gave me a drink". (8) "For His disciples had gone away into the city to buy food". (9) "then the woman of Samaria said to Him, how is it that you, being a Jew, ask a drink from me, a Samaritan woman? For the Jews have no dealings with Samaritans". (10) "Jesus answered and said to her; if you knew the gift of God, and who it is who says to you, give me a drink, you would have asked him, and he would have given you living water". Note; look at (10) Very close. When Jesus said to her, if you knew the gift of God. Here he is plainly telling her, if she only knew who He was. He is the Redeemer, the Savior of the world, the Spirit of the Almighty God. The woman did not know this. If she did, as Jesus said, she would have asked Him, for a drink of His Spirit, as referred to as living water. This of course would be her salvation through Christ. But the woman did not have a clue of what He spoke of. (11) "the woman said to him, sir, you have nothing to draw with, and the well is deep. Where then do you get the

living water"? (12) "are you greater than our father Jacob, who gave us the well, and drank from it himself, as well as his sons and his livestock"? Note; once again, the woman does not have a clue, Jesus is her Redeemer. (13) "Jesus answered and said to her, whosoever drinks of this water will thirst again". Note; Jesus is just simply stating a fact. That is, this water is of the physical world. (14) "but whosoever drinks of the water that I shall give him will never thirst. But the water that I shall give him will become in him a fountain of water springing up into everlasting life". Note; in this verse, Jesus is plainly stating a Spiritual knowledge. The knowledge that He is the Holy Spirit. He is the Redeemer. He is her salvation. If she would take a drink, or receive His Spirit, she would live forever. (15) "the woman said to him, Sir, give me this water, that I may not thirst, nor come here to draw". Note; the woman still does not have a clue what Jesus is talking about. (16) "Jesus said to her, go, call your husband, and come here". Note; pay close attention to these next scriptures. This is where my point will be made. Remember, Jesus is the Holy Spirit in an anointed flesh vessel. The Holy Spirit of course is the Almighty God Jehovah, our Father in Heaven. Therefore, He already knows this woman has no certificate of marriage. (17) "the woman answered and said, I have no husband. Jesus said to her, you have well said. I have no husband". Note; in this verse, Jesus and the woman both are acknowledging, she is not married by Holy matrimony, with a certified certificate by law. (18) 'For you have had five husbands, and the one you now have is not your husband, in that you spoke truly" (NKJV).

In the first part of (18), Jesus is plainly stating a spiritual connection of a bond when He says to her, "You have had five husbands, and the one whom you now have is not your husband." This means that she was never married by the law with a marriage certificate. But she was married by the spiritual bond, as Jesus plainly stated. The Bible teaches us in Matthew 18:18, "whatsoever you shall bind on earth shall be bound in Heaven: and whatsoever ye shall loose on earth shall be loosed in Heaven." This plainly tells me that we are spiritually bonded to whatever we do on Earth as flesh. The only way to be set free from this bond is through Jesus Christ, our redeemer. This, of course, must happen before we leave planet Earth. Jesus the Christ is the anointed Spirit of God Jehovah, our Father in Heaven. If it is still not clear to you, read the entire chapter of Matthew 18, and the entire chapter of John 4.

We may have often heard that marriage is a giving and receiving commitment—more commonly expressed as "give and take." What we may not have heard is that, if both—I did say both—would focus more on the giving, then, of course, both would be overwhelmed with the receiving. Many of us may look at scripture and see it as a one-way street. Let's look at Ephesians 5:22: "Wives, submit yourselves unto to your own husbands, as unto the Lord" (NKJV). Perhaps some women may look at this verse and say, "there is no way that man is going to rule over me." She may even add something like, "he doesn't have the sense God gave a chicken, there's just no way!" (Well, I just had to put that in there!) The point is this—if this woman is correct about her husband, then perhaps he doesn't have good sense. But, if she and he were both united in Spirit with Christ, they would truly understand the scripture. No one has the right or the authority by the Word of God to rule or to be a demanding spouse over the other. This is not what scripture is teaching us. Look at Ephesians 5:23–25: "For the husband is head of the wife, as also Christ is the head of the church; and he is the Savior the body. Therefore, just as the church is subject to Christ, so let the wives be to their own husbands in everything. Husbands, love your wives, just as Christ also loved the church and gave himself for her" (NKJV). (Or, "instead of her," "it", as the King James Version reads.)

Since I truly don't know if everyone can understand what is said in Ephesians 5:23–25, I will do my best to explain. First, remember this, Adam was created first. God then reached into the side of Adam and removed what was necessary to create woman. (This is a mystery you may or may not understand. Woman is often referred to as man's better half). Eve did tempt Adam, and he did eat of the forbidden fruit. Even so, it was Adam's will as well as Eve's to eat from the forbidden fruit, or to sin against God. With that said, keep in mind what I am going to say. Ephesians 5:23–25 simply admonishes a wife to pay close attention to her husband's words concerning the Word of God. Why would the Bible, or the Word of God, give this responsibility to the man, the husband? Well, who was created first, and who was persuaded by the other to sin? Now I know a young man, smitten, and deeply in love, is going to do whatever he can to please his woman. This is the way it ought to be, even for an old man, but with spiritual guidance! This is the reason an Adam, or the husband of a family, is given the responsibility for spiritual guidance concerning the Word of God. You think not? Let's just look at verse 23: "for the husband is the head of the wife, even as Christ is the head of the church: and he is the savior of the body." This is what I see in plain English. The husband is responsible; he is the head of the wife in spiritual knowledge. Spiritual knowledge—the Word of God—is Christ! Therefore, Christ is the head, or the beginning, of the church. This knowledge of Christ is salvation of a body, or a family. Therefore, God has placed man (the husband) above woman (the wife) for this responsibility.

Now, if a man doesn't have this sense of responsibility for his salvation, or his family's, then the woman must step up to the plate. That's about as plainly as I can put it. Ephesians 5:24 reads, "therefore, as the church is subject to Christ, so let the wives be to their own husbands in everything." This, of course, is with good sense, and within the Word of God. Verse 25 reads, "husbands, love your wives, even as Christ also loved the church, and gave himself for her." Gentleman, did you hear those words? You are not the master of the home, or your wife. You are her servant, and the family's as well. Ladies, did you hear those words? You are not a slave to your husband! But, if it is God's will in spiritual guidance, please keep an open ear to your husband's comments.

In the Bible, the Word of God, there is great knowledge and wisdom. Read and study your Bible; it is a book of life. As you read, listen for the voice of God. He will speak to you. If He spoke with His prophets verbally, men of flesh and earthly spirit, but of great faith, He will surely speak with His adopted children. For His Spirit is dwelling in you. Listen for His Spirit within you, then clearly, in your mind and heart, hear Him speak.

Praise be to God.

The Holidays

Here in America, as well as around the world, we take our holidays seriously. Sadly, the question we may ask ourselves is, do we take them truly seriously, or just traditionally joyfully? Seriously concerned, I'm thinking only of a few holidays; these are, New Year's, Christmas, Easter, and Thanksgiving.

A New Year's celebration is a time when we celebrate the ending of the past year and the beginning of a new year. Spiritually minded, we must realize that what has passed is gone forever, and what we hope is to come may not come. The Bible teaches us that yesterday is gone, and tomorrow might not come; there is no promise. This, now, is to say that today is the only day of life. We cannot change the history of yesterday. This may always be embedded in the minds of many. Whether it be the history of good deeds or of evil, what is done is done, completed. What we can do is improve today, the only day of life. Yesterday is gone, and tomorrow may not come, so now is the time. Realizing this truth, we can say that every day is a Sabbath day. How can I say this? John 4:24. Think about this, please. If yesterday is gone, and there is no promise of tomorrow, then all we have is today. John 4:24 reads, "God is Spirit, and we must worship Him, in Spirit and in truth" (NKJV). With this in my mind, every day is a Sabbath. Happy New Year!

The Christmas celebration here in America is a time when some celebrate a mythical fantasy, while others celebrate a spiritual awareness of the day our Savior was born. Some of us may have awareness of both, and celebrate with the spirits from a bottle, for good cheer and happy moments. Whatever the case may be, whatever is truly in your heart, we must never forget Christmas is a celebration of the birth of Christ.

Many of us as Americans forget that the First Amendment of our Great American Constitution is for all Americans. No one has the right to defile that great First Amendment. I can boldly say, without having taken a survey, that most Americans celebrate Christmas as a religious holiday. Some may disagree. This is your God-given right, and your American constitutional right. By the justifying words of our Constitution, under the laws of God and man, in respect for all, perhaps we all should use a little common sense—either silently disagree, or verbally disagree in a peaceful and lawful manner. If someone's religious belief or action is unsupportive to the well-being of others, bring it to a court of law. We should not waste money and time of others for our selfish and so-called religious beliefs. This would truly be respected as Americans for all Americans.

Some of us, as Christians, or whatever we care to call ourselves in Christ Jesus, disagree with Christmas as well. I sincerely understand why some may feel this way. First of all, I know December 25 has never been recorded as the birthday of Christ. The Bible, and many other historic documents, do not record the date of the birth of Christ. This day is totally unknown to us as believers in Christ, or anyone else. The fact still remains, He was here! Not only the Bible, but many other books and historical documents claim the life of Jesus Christ. We, as Americans, no matter what beliefs we hold in value, should always recognize December 25 as a celebration of the birth of our salvation through the life, death, burial, and resurrection of Jesus Christ. To disagree with the celebration of Christmas, as a believer in Christ, in my opinion, one would unwillingly support the voice of an unbeliever. Truly, it is not when we celebrate Christmas, but how we celebrate Christmas, as the birth of Christ our Savior.

*

A Christmas Poem

It is said, on the twenty-fifth of
December baby Jesus was born,
As we know, in the town of Bethlehem in a crib so warm,
With the wise men to greet Him and
the people to meet Him,
They rejoiced to the world for our Savior was born.
Baby Jesus lay still in His cradle that night, with
a glow of purity, like the star in the night.
The people brought gifts and kneeled in prayer,
for our Savior Jesus had now been there.
With the myth of Santa and all his cheer,
let's not forget Jesus, for He was here.
He came as our Savior on this blessed night; give
thanks to our Lord that there was such a sight,
The sight of purity and goodness in heart, and
salvation to man, which He fourth brought.
So think of young Jesus at this time of the year, and
think of young Jesus throughout your new year,
For man young Jesus should be his cheer,
So have a Merry Christmas, and a Happy New Year.

My Lord gave me these words back in 1972. I had just begun to read His Word for the first time in my life. At that time I was quite blind to His Word and the mysteries of life. I was twenty-one years of age and dumb as a pet rock. I truly believe now that, at that time of my life, God placed me in His heated forge and began to form me into the man in Christ I am today. I must have been one tough piece of work, for I too wandered in the wilderness for forty years. I can surely relate to the Jews of the Old Testament in their search for the Promised Land as well. Merry Christmas!

On the holiday of Easter, the very young excitedly look for Easter eggs and baskets of candy. These precious young souls have not a clue of the significance of this celebration. Sadly to say, many of us as adults may be poorly informed as well.

The common terminology for this day would truly be Passover. Many believe the word *Easter* comes from the name *Eoster*, an Anglo Saxon goddess. Some believe it comes from the word *eostur*, the Norse word for spring.

Easter falls between March 23 and April 26. The date each year is set for the first Sunday after the first full moon that occurs after March 21. This date is one of the first days of spring. Long ago, Easter was celebrated during the same time that the Jews celebrated Passover—the fourteenth day of the month of Nisan, by the Jewish calendar. Through the years, Easter was changed to Sunday, the day now known as the Christian Sabbath. Easter may be the oldest Christian celebration, other then the Sabbath. Even so, Easter wasn't always celebrated as the Easter Sunday service we know today. The earliest known celebration was Pasch. This celebration was recognized between the second and fourth centuries. The celebrations of Pasch combined both the death and the resurrection of Jesus at the same time. Today these two events have been split up between Good Friday and Easter Sunday, as we celebrate today.

Our Christian celebration of Easter is truly in common with the Jewish celebration of Passover. For Jews, Passover is the celebration of their freedom from bondage of the Egyptians. Exodus 12:7–13 tells us the story of how the Angel of Death passed over the homes of the Egyptians and Jewish people. Any Jews who had splashed the blood of an animal sacrifice on the top and sides of the doorframes of their homes were saved, or spared, from the Angel of Death.

To my understanding of scripture, my opinion of the blood sacrifice on the doorframes leading into the homes would be symbolic to the death of Christ. How? Christ is our Passover. His death, His shed blood, covers our sin. Therefore, the Angel of Death cannot harm us. His blood is on the doorframe of Heaven; it is our sign we may enter. This, of course, is my understanding of mind and heart; the idea is not in the words of scripture.

In today's day and age, Passover, or Easter, may not be seen as the serious celebrations they are. Many of us have a picture of innocence, but it's not the innocence of Christ we see. Many of us have a picture of a joyful time, but it was not joyful for the physical form of Christ. Many of us have a picture of the Easter Bunny in a fantasy of Easter, but it was no fantasy for Christ. Many of us will dress up and look our best for Easter Sunday service, but Christ was undressed, beaten unmerciful, and nailed to a cross. He took the blame for our sins. This is the service He gave us.

Easter may truly be a time of innocence for very young children. But I pray that, as they grow into the knowledge of life, they may also grow in the knowledge of His Word, the Bible. Happy Easter!

The first Thanksgiving celebration was in 1621. The first Thanksgiving of the pilgrims and the Wampanoag Indians was more like a harvest festival. This first harvest festival, or Thanksgiving as we call it today, did not start an annual celebration, although through the following century it was celebrated occasionally. After the Revolutionary War, in 1777, Americans did celebrate Thanksgiving. But, even at this time, it was not declared a national holiday. It was declared a national holiday in 1863. Abraham Lincoln proclaimed the last Thursday in November Thanksgiving Day. But then, in 1939, President Franklin Roosevelt changed the date once again; he declared the fourth Thursday in November as Thanksgiving Day. This is truly when a traditional thanksgiving was celebrated as we know it today.

The pilgrims who settled in America were truly the origin of Thanksgiving—not only the first souls who stepped onto what was to be American soil, but also the many who followed in the centuries to come. The early settlers of America, toward the end of the seventeenth century, brought with them the Geneva Bible. This Bible was one of the earliest translated manuscript recorded in English. Noted for its easy reading and many references, this Bible may have been commonly taught in our early settlement schools.

In the year 1553, Mary Tudor, commonly known as Bloody Mary, became Queen of England. When she became queen, she was determined to abolish all Protestant teaching in England, and to claim Roman Catholicism as the only religion. The Protestant preachers of the Word of God were forced to leave England.

The Protestant preachers and scholars who were forced to leave England traveled to Geneva, Switzerland. There, in the year 1560, these men created and published the English translation of the Holy scriptures known as the Geneva Bible. This Bible made its way to England and Scotland. It was greatly appreciated, even after the King James translation of 1611.

With the knowledge of a little history, and the thoughts of the Christian mind, I truly am thankful. I am thankful for the many men, women, and children who traveled to this land. They came with dreams of a new life in a land where they could express their spiritual awareness opinions openly and boldly—an awareness given to them from a book called the Geneva Bible. With the knowledge they learned from the Geneva Bible, the Spirit of God as a seed was conceived in this new land. With time, great pain and suffering, and the travail of birth, America was born. America is a nation born with Christian blood flowing through her veins, a nation whose early righteous laws expressed the fear and the love of God. America! We say in God we trust, we pray God bless America, we pledge one nation under God, but how do we truly stand as Americans this day? Wake up, sleepy Christians! Give thanks to God our Father today, for yesterday is gone, and America's tomorrow may not come. Happy Thanksgiving!

Praise be to God.

Summary

Hopefully you have read *My Study* in its entirety. If you have, I am quite sure you can understand why I say that I am no different than anyone else on this planet. I did live a life of open and bold sin, and still claimed the love of God. I lived what the Bible calls a double-standard life. God did love me even then. But, did I truly love Him, or much less, even know Him? The only reason I am the man in Christ I am today is that I have received the love of God.

We have all heard the saying, God works in mysterious ways. I have to say I can truly understand and believe that statement. Even though I have gone through the fire, as God has forged me into the man I am, I had not a clue of His work in me, or His finished product.

It all began about ten years ago. A gentleman and his wife came to my house to spread the good news. This, of course, was the Word of God concerning the gospels. As we spoke of one topic of scripture that explained Jesus the Son of God, I could plainly see we were not on the same page. My visitor's understanding of Christ and my understanding were completely different. He told me Jesus was not God, but *a god*. This statement shocked me. It did not make me angry, but it did make me curious. I had always been taught that Jesus was the Son of God, but yet He was God in the flesh. This, of course, would be the familiar Holy Trinity. As I tried to explain my understanding of a trinity, he did not buy my understanding. I understood why. It was because I could not explain a trinity other than to say, He was the Son of God, but yet, He was God in the flesh. It's a God thing; we just have to believe it.

As the years and months passed, this gentleman continued to visit me. During this time I had begun to study the scripture to prove my point of a trinity. What was truly a great help in my study was the fact that I had acquired a new Bible. I had gone to a family function and had been speaking with a dear and sweet cousin of mine. She also was of the same religion as this gentleman who had visited with me for many years. At this family function, she and I spoke briefly of the scriptures. She told me she would send me a copy of the Bible that she read. This was the New World Translation.

I love my cousin dearly, even though we were not very close through the years. The love of your family is always there. This is the same in the heart of God for the adopted children, as well as others of this world. The bottom line, yet the top line—Christ Jesus is our Savior. I believe it doesn't truly matter what religion we might follow, as long as we truly know Christ is our Savior. Some, of course, may disagree.

After I received the New World Translation, I plainly understood in my mind that I must search many Bible translations. I sincerely believed God did use man to write His scripture from the given Words to the prophets, mainly because it was the words of God spoken to man in verbal conversation. Through the centuries, the Word of God has been translated into many languages, many times. Translation from Hebrew and Greek to any language is very difficult to accurately accomplish. I believe this is why many Bible texts differ. I truly don't care if one's opinions at this day and age comes from the Dead Sea Scrolls, or any other script. It is very difficult to translate.

As I studied scripture from the different Bible translations, I learned to put my religious doctrines back in the box they had come out of. This is truly when I began to see scripture at face value. As I diligently sought God and His Word, I still could not prove a trinity. After years and countless hours, I found something more, something greater than a trinity. I found the only one and true God—the all-knowing, all-loving, all-merciful, Almighty God, my Father in Heaven.

My God is a just and righteous God. He does not willingly send anyone to eternal damnation. The Bible teaches us that "the wages of sin is death." Think about this! If you work for a company, you will receive wages for your work. In life, if we live a sinful and unjust life, what we have worked for in our lives, are the wages we receive. If it is sinful, the payment is death. You would have earned your justified wages. Christ Jesus is willing to accept those sinful wages and pay the death penalty of our sin, for us, with His life. All we have to do is believe that He will.

In this life we are body, soul, and spirit. I said in this little book, *My Study*, that your soul is a record of your life. As I was speaking with my older sister just moments ago, as I worked on this chapter, she explained to me how she had been taught. Your soul is your mind, your will, and your emotions. I told her I could agree with those explanations completely—the reason being, your mind, your will, and your emotions are etched into the history of your existence, which is a confirmed history of your life. This, of course, is a record of your life.

A few years ago, as I was driving down the highway, I was thinking about scripture concerning body, soul, and spirit. As I thought about scripture deeply, I still could not understand, by scripture, what the soul actually was. Suddenly, in my Spirit in Christ, I heard the voice of God. This was not a verbal conversation, but it was a conversation, and very real. The Lord told me, "Your soul is like an SD card. [This would be a memory card.] As I heard these words in my Spirit, I said out loud, "Lord, what are you talking about? What do you mean an SD card?" Moments later, I had a vision in my mind of my digital camera. The Lord explained to me that the battery in my camera is the energy of life, the spirit He has given me. The camera, as my body, contained the life He gave me, and the SD card was the record of my life. I said out loud once again, "Lord, what is this all about?" Moments later, as I drove along in wonder, the Lord explained in pure detail. He said to me in my Spirit of Christ, "Your camera is your body, the batteries are the short life you live here on Earth. Your SD card is the everlasting memory of your life." He then plainly explained to me that, for those who come to Him through the life of Jesus Christ, He would delete that SD card of all unrighteousness. This would mean the unrighteousness is lost and forgotten forever. He then said, "If your camera takes pictures of filth, of sin, this is who you are." He then said that, if you come to Him, He would delete that filth from within you. (This, I believe, even now as an adopted child of God: If, or when we might happen to sin, He will delete it if we have truly surrendered to Christ.

We, the people of the natural world, are led by the natural spirit. But if we should hear the Grace Age gospel, taught by the apostle Paul, which was given to him by revelation from Christ, and we believe, then we are saved by grace and nothing else. Then by faith, we are led by the Spirit of Christ. This is truly when we can establish a relationship with our Father in Heaven, for we will be like Christ, His anointed earthly vessel or Son. We, too, are His earthly adopted sons and daughters. As it was for Christ, the Almighty Holy Spirit is our Father in Heaven, and not just the God of creation.

By the renewing of mind and spirit, we are transformed into the Spirit of Christ. We are now one in Christ, as Christ is one in the Father. We are now adopted into the family of God, our Father in Heaven.

Praise be to God.

Closing Words

First, I seriously pray that I have not offended anyone with my thoughts and opinions. It is not my intent to offend anyone. It is only my passion to express what I truly believe scripture teaches. For the past few years, as I diligently searched the scriptures for understanding, I grew with great excitement and a true passion to understand the Word of God. Many of my friends and relatives may have thought I was a little thrown off, as I desperately needed to express my passion. The Word of God teaches us, "Ask, and it shall be given you; seek, and ye shall find; knock, and it shall be opened unto you." What I have found is truly a passion that must be expressed openly and boldly.

A very long time ago, in prayer with my Father of Heaven, I asked, "What can I do to serve you, Lord? What can I do to be called a good and faithful servant? I am not a well-educated man. I am not a preacher. I don't have a TV or radio show to serve you, Lord, so what can I possibly do?"

Through the years and many hours searching the Word of God, I realized, then understood, a very important message: It's not what we can do in the flesh with regard to works of good merit, it is truly what we do in the Spirit of Christ. If yesterday is gone, and tomorrow holds no promise, it is today we worship. John 4:24 tells us, "God is Spirit, and those who worship Him must worship in spirit and in truth" (NKJV). This would be every day of our given lives here on planet Earth, in the Spirit of Christ, in the truth of His Word. Does this mean for us to literally get down on our knees every day and recite some prayer that we've heard, or have been taught? Now, I don't think so. You may do so if it pleases you, or if you feel it pleases God. But I truly believe that to worship Him is to live of His statute and to keep His commandments in your mind and in your heart. Jesus said in John 14:15, "If you love Me, keep My commandments" (NKJV). Does this mean we should never break a commandment? Willingly, of course not! But does this mean, that it is possible for a man of flesh, other than Christ, not to break a commandment? If this is so, then perhaps God would have waited for this man to be born. Then He would not have had to come to His creation, as His creation, the only begotten of the flesh, His anointed earthly vessel, for the redemption of our sins. No, Christ has paid in full; this is why we are set free from our sins.

If you personally know me, as a friend or relative, and have not seen or spoken with me for quite some time, you may be surprised at my thoughts and opinions. You may say to someone, "Lookee here, old- Bubba has found religion! I can't believe that!" Well, if this were to be so, you would most certainly be incorrect. I do not believe that I have found religion, for I have found something greater than religion. In the darkness of this world, with the guiding light of Christ, I have found my way home. My Father has welcomed me with open arms and a great celebration. His love for me has never failed. His excitement at my return is full of great joy. As we celebrate together in Spirit as one, I have truly found my relationship with my Father of Heaven as His adopted son.

When Adam and Eve lost their spiritual home when they disobeyed God. They had lost their way in the darkness of a sinful world. The knowledge of good and evil is one thing. But to truly understand how to make the choice between good and evil is quite a different story. Without the constant care, the guiding light of God our Father of Heaven, the demanding will of the flesh may lead us in the darkness of this sinful world. This is to say, we are lost! We are blind! Read the scriptures of the Holy Bible. Look for the guiding light of Christ. He is truly our only way back home.

I pray that, from this little book, you have seen scripture as mighty Words and gained a true understanding of one Spirit. We are one in Christ, as Christ is one in our Father. All in all.

Praise be to God, my Father in Heaven.